The Open Gate

Don Ian Smith

Broadman Press
Nashville, Tennessee

© Copyright 1989 • Broadman Press
All rights reserved
4259-19
ISBN: 0-8054-5919-7

Dewey Decimal Classification: 240
Subject Heading: DEVOTIONAL LITERATURE
Library of Congress Catalog Card Number: 89-37398
Printed in the United States of America

Unless otherwise noted, all Scripture quotations are taken from the King James Version of the Bible.

Scripture quotations marked RSV are taken from the *Revised Standard Version of the Bible* copyright 1946, 1952, © 1971, 1973 by the National Council of Churches of Christ in the U.S.A., and used by permission.

Scripture quotations marked Phillips are reprinted with permission of Macmillan Publishing Co., Inc. from J. B. Phillips: *The New Testament in Modern English,* Revised Edition. © J. B. Phillips 1958, 1960, 1972.

Library of Congress Cataloging-in-Publication Data

Smith, Don Ian, 1918-
    The open gate / Don Ian Smith.
      p.   cm.
    ISBN 0-8054-5919-7
    1. Nature—Religious aspects—Christianity—Meditations.
I. Title.
BT695.5.S635   1989   89-37398
242—dc20   CIP

Contents

1. The Open Gate — 5
2. Fireweed and Ashes — 12
3. In All Generations — 19
4. Cabbages — 24
5. Top for the Tree — 29
6. Pruning Peach Trees — 35
7. Prayer on the Run — 40
8. When the Rocks Talk — 47
9. Square Watermelons — 52
10. Every Valley Lifted Up — 59
11. Any Bush Will Do! — 66
12. Streetlights and Headlights — 71
13. The Turkey Trap — 76
14. Chasing Donkeys — 84
15. Cooking with Leftovers — 92
16. Fences — 100
17. Little Dog—Big Sled — 106
18. Frogs and Pollywogs — 113
19. A Bucket of Muddy Water — 120
20. Little Tiger Cat — 125

1
The Open Gate

In a prominent place on our living room wall we have hung a painting. The artist is a personal friend and retired forester, Walt Sundell. I am not an art critic; the painting may not be great art. But it does have a simple and beautiful message. It is a western scene, typical of an Idaho cattle ranch. A rider approaches the picturesque pole fence, and the gate is open.

I look at the picture and remember with pleasure the times in my life when I have appreciated an open gate. It is the opposite of frustration and disappointment. It speaks of friendship, it beckons to adventure, it is a word of hope.

It is a wonderful symbol of the Christian faith. Jesus speaks of Himself as the door of the sheepfold (gate would be very appropriate) through which the sheep go in and out and find pasture. It is an open gate; it is an invitation to the adventure of green pastures and mountain meadows and the comfort of a place of rest and retreat when the day's adventuring is done (John 10:9).

There is two-way traffic through an open gate. It

speaks of relationships that are not one sided. Someone wants to be our neighbor, wants to know us better, would like us to come in and sit a while and share a cup. The need for bolted doors and padlocked gates is a sad commentary on our modern society. An open gate is surely a thing of joy and a symbol of hope.

Properly understood, Christianity is a faith that opens gates. I'm sure that is what Jesus intended it to be. Many religions are constantly closing gates, putting restrictions on life, and emphasizing the negative rather than lifting up the positive. They build walls and put up signs that say, Do Not Enter. Jesus comes to bring an abundant life, an expanding adventure. He knocks on the door and promises to come in and eat with anyone who has the faith to open the door.

On a cattle range where I used to do some riding we had a management fence, so we could save some of the higher range for the cattle to use in the late summer. When the grasses on the lower range had been well grazed and some of the lower springs and water holes had dried up, the cattle began to work their way toward the high country. When it was time to move to the higher ranges the old cows would already be in the vicinity of the gate where we let them through. It was always a pleasure to open that gate and see the eagerness with which they crowded through, often frisking and bucking in their pleasure. They knew it was a passage to greener grass, more trees and shade for hot afternoons, creeks and coulees to explore. It was the satisfaction of their hopes and needs—a better life.

We, like the cattle, often find life growing barren and dry. Grass is cropped short; water holes that stored the

THE OPEN GATE

spring runoff have become stale, muddy, and bad tasting. We long for streams and springs instead of the catch ponds of the low, flat country. We seek an open gate to the high range. And the wonder of the Christian faith is its power to open gates that will admit us to the green pastures and still waters of a better life.

Our faith in Christ opens many gates, and three in particular: it opens a gate to a closer understanding and relationship with God; it opens a gate to better understanding and fellowship with other people; it opens the gate to the future.

All people believe something. There are many forms of religion and some very limited ideas held in the name of Christianity. Most lesser religions see life as a series of closed gates and religion as a constant effort on our part to open the gates by ourselves. We don't like the gates; our human efforts are insufficient to open them, and we despair.

I was pastor for many years in an area where rancher members of my church often lived on mountain roads in open-range country. Driving to some of the homes meant going through many fences where the gates had to be kept closed, and some of the gates were hard to open. I remember one rather isolated ranch, several miles up a creek, where there were eight gates on the road. We nicknamed the creek Gate Creek. We had a joke about someone who always wanted to drive, because the passenger seat was the "gate seat." That person had to get out to open the gates.

Religion as our search for God is like this. There are gates of mystery to be opened by rituals; gates of ignorance to be opened by study; gates of sinfulness to be opened by the keeping of strict moral law. But in Christianity God is searching for us even more than we are seeking Him. Christ comes to open the gates. God so loved the world that He sent His Son to open gates, reconciling the world to Himself. That's the good news of Christmas. God and sinners reconciled—gates opened wide.

I well remember my sense of pleasure one day when driving up "Gate Creek." I happened along just in time to drive behind the man who lived there and was on his way home. He opened all the gates for me. And when we arrived at the ranch house where the yard, house, and ranch building were all protected by a good cow-proof fence, the owner's own son came out and opened wide the gate for us. What a sense of welcome! What a symbol of our Christian hope: Gates—often heavy gates with which we struggle—are opened wide for us by One who welcomes us to share His hospitality.

Religion that sees life as a struggle on our part to open gates by our own human wisdom, moral goodness, or faithfulness in rituals offers us a struggle we must finally lose. Luther says it so well in the great hymn "A Mighty Fortress Is Our God": "Did we in our own strength confide,/Our striving would be losing;/Were not the right Man on our side,/The Man of God's own choosing."

I like to think of the prodigal son (Luke 15) as a young man growing up in a large pleasant ranch house. Like many such homes it is surrounded by a fence that needs to be kept shut and locked. But all members of the family, and even the hired men, have keys. The young man grows up and believes he no longer needs his parents and their love. Family traditions annoy him; he will be independent. The prodigal leaves the home, and in his self-confidence throws away his key. Later on, tired, destitute, and hungry, he is coming home. The son realizes even the hired men are better off than he is, and he remembers the gate. Even a hired man would have a key but he, the son, will have trouble getting in.

And then that joyous moment of truth: he doesn't need a key. The Father himself has unlocked the gate and is running to welcome the boy. The son is not a hired man, and he never will be. But how often many of us mope along in our religious life as if we are employees of a large, impersonal corporation instead of very special friends of the chairman of the board. And we sometimes give our gifts as if we were paying our dues instead of bringing a love offering into our Father's house. Christ opens the gate to a fuller and more intimate relationship with a loving and caring God.

Christ opens the gates in fences that separate us from other people. It is so easy to let hurts and misunderstanding build barriers between us and our neighbors. Loving the unlovable is not something that just comes naturally.

I remember early in my ministry an older man of prominence in our community who saw things differently than I, took a strong dislike of me, and hurt me deeply. He didn't like me, and I certainly didn't like him. Circumstances made it inevitable that we had to work with each other from time to time and serve on certain committees together. My dislike for him and my resentment were so strong that it was an emotional drain: it was hurting me.

Then one Sunday, when on vacation in a town a long

way from home, I attended a church of the denomination to which the man belonged—different from my own. During the service my thoughts turned to him and pondered the fact that Christ had died for that rascal. If Christ died for him, could I do less than pray for him, which I did. I prayed for his well-being, for his family, and for his prosperity. It certainly didn't make us friends, but it took the bitterness out of my life. Next time I saw the man I stretched out my hand in greeting. He did not but said: "Is it necessary for us to shake hands?" It wasn't. But now I could see him in meetings and at community functions; see him prosper, discuss community issues, and keep my cool. I was not upset by him and his attitude.

We don't love people because we are good, broadminded, and understanding folks—we are not that nice. But we can love because Christ has first loved us in spite of our meanness. He can help me love my crooked neighbor with all my crooked heart. He goes around opening gates that I have shut because of my small-mindedness and lack of understanding. This is the power that can heal broken homes, broken church fellowship in a congregation, and broken business and community relationships. It is a great day when you participate in a crowded communion service and find yourself beside that person you don't like. You find you are each reaching out your hand with the same need and the same hunger for the same symbols of Jesus' body and blood.

It is our faith in Christ that can open to us the gate to the future. Certainly as we grow older, we find we are never going back to good things that are past. We soon discover we cannot be sustained by memories, lovely as they may be, but only by faith in and hope for the future.

THE OPEN GATE

As I visit with older people, I find two different ways of viewing the future. One way, sadly too common, sees the future as unknown but bound to get worse. This view is inevitable if we trust only in our own strength, which with aging is being constantly reduced. If we trust only our own strength, we must be filled with fear rather than faith.

But this is not the true story. The way to the future is not through a locked door or a closed gate which we must somehow manage to open. As we are less and less able to cope, we find we are not alone. Of course, we do not know the way into the future, but we do not need to know the way for we know the Guide. And instead of a blind alley we see an open gate. We worship on the first day of the week to celebrate the resurrection, and each Sunday we are reminded that we are the Easter people, looking always to the future and never the past, looking to the sunrise of eternity, even down to our last day in the present life. What a good feeling it is, after a long, hard, and rewarding day of riding the high country, to approach the homeplace in the friendly shadows of evening time, to see a welcoming light in the ranch-house window and a wide-open gate.

2
Fireweed and Ashes

Just a few years after the explosion of Mount Saint Helens on May 8, 1980 in the state of Washington, Betty and I toured that scene of devastation. It was an awesome sight. There is nothing in our normal life experience that can help us grasp the magnitude of the force that blew the mountain apart, flattened a great forest for miles around, and scattered volcanic dust over several states. In a matter of moments on the day of that blast, a huge area became a wasteland. One is at first impressed by the power of the destruction.

But very quickly, after the first shock of seeing so much that was destroyed, one becomes aware of a power far greater than the explosion that ripped the top off the mountain. Almost everywhere we looked we saw fireweed, not only growing but blooming—creating seeds to further enhance the recovery of the land. As we saw the fireweed, growing among the ashes, we soon began to notice many other signs of life forms that were already evident on what had seemed a dead landscape. Some birds had returned along with a number of other species. Out of the ashes there was new life.

FIREWEED AND ASHES

The power of destruction had come suddenly with such force that it had captured the attention of the world. But the greater power, the power of life that is stronger than death, the power of healing, God's power to restore, was coming quietly as a sunrise. Without smoke or rumbling, with no great way of catching the world's attention, but with acres of blossoms, the fireweed was proclaiming a message of hope. The future is with the fireweed.

Fireweed is a spectacular, beautiful plant with varieties from one to seven feet tall. Long stalks of pink to purple blooms give the impression of a plant that is almost all blossom; and growing as it does in great profusion, it will turn a burned-over area into a solid sea of color. In addition to the beauty that it brings, its palatable leaves and stalks provide forage for many creatures such as deer and elk, encouraging their return to a damaged land. In their fine little book *The Plants of Yellowstone Park*, W. B. McDougall and Herma A. Baggley discuss Fireweed of the Evening Primrose Family: "It is called Fireweed because of its rapid growth following a devastating fire. . . . During the 'blitz' of London and other English cities in World War II, Fireweed was one of the two plants to appear en masse among the devastation and ruin, comforting and cheering the confused and weary residents."

In the same quiet and unassuming way in which the fireweed grows, God speaks to us again in the beauty and wonder of the Christmas story. On our streets and in our homes the symbolic decorations bloom; in the air are the Christmas carols, speaking again of that great power of the love of God, reaching into our world with a message of hope: "O'er all the weary world." God is making sure that we do not forget his love for us, that we do remember our love for each other. We give gifts—not because they are needed, but to remind one another that we care. We write letters sharing our news. If we are out of touch, we want to be in touch. The estranged seek reconciliation; the wanderer comes home; ties of family and friendship are cherished. Something wonderful is growing and blossoming even in the ashes of discouragement, and in the "dark streets shineth the everlasting light."

Recently I was preparing our annual Christmas letter, and there kept coming to my mind the picture of the fireweed in the ashes: this symbol of hope in the midst of devastation. The coming of Christmas each year is like the fireweed, quietly, persistently, constantly proclaiming the awesome power of God to restore, to heal, to bring life and hope no matter what the powers of destruction may have done. It is a power that works so gently, like the coming of springtime, that we sometimes forget that it is the greatest force in all creation. We live in a world where there are great forces of destruction—great powers of evil. But of all people Christians should always remember that because of the very nature of God, revealed in the One whose birth we celebrate at Christmas, there is hope. That is God's way.

"Now when Jesus was born in Bethlehem of Judaea in the days of Herod the king" (Matt. 2:1)—that's when He was born, in the days of Herod, a horrid, brutal king and dictator. These were dark days of pain and suffering such as few have ever known in modern times. Into this world of devastation and destruction a Child was born, a Child of love and hope—new life to heal the pain and devastation. The future is with the Child, not with Herod or any of his kind then or now. That is God's way, for God so loved the world.

FIREWEED AND ASHES

It is important for Christians in our time to proclaim the gospel of hope. Because of the power of the atom bomb, because the news media can constantly keep us aware of the spectacular and noisy instances of destruction, it is easy for us to forget that God's power of restoration, of growth, of life, of creation itself is always at work and is much stronger than any short-lived atomic blast or even an earthquake or volcano.

A problem in our time, even among avowed Christians, is a tendency to focus on the powers of destruction and forget the gospel of hope. We hear talk about human ability to destroy the earth as if somehow God has lost control of creation. We hear talk of nuclear winter and so much emphasis on devastation that a generation of our young people are living in fear—fear that takes away their dreams of the future, despair that can even lead to suicide, or a retreat into a meaningless life of drug use.

Realism is important if we are to deal with our problems, but honest realism does not just see the ashes of evil. It sees beyond the ashes to the fireweed and the blossoms. On the darkest night, it sees a star in the east: "For unto us a child is born." It is so easy to see the smoke of a forest fire or the devastation of a flood that we can overlook the greater power of millions and millions of grass roots that are helping to make new topsoil, the gentle power of a tree root that can help to crack a rock.

Destruction is noisy and calls attention to itself. The soldiers of Herod, searching the streets of Bethlehem and brutally murdering the children, would have caused a noisy and terrible event (Matt. 2:16). But in the stillness of the night the Child of hope was born. "How silently, how silently/The wondrous gift [was] giv'n!" And just as quietly Joseph "took the child and his mother by night and departed into Egypt." A power far greater than the evil power of Herod was on the side of the Child.

That is God's way. It is tragic if we in our time are so caught up in the sounds of destruction, if we give our thinking over to fear and despair, that we lose our contact with the quiet powers of creation and fail to proclaim the gospel of hope that is the heart of the Christmas message and the foundation of our faith.

All great Christian preaching, patterned after the preaching of the apostle Paul, has proclaimed the gospel of hope—hope that can lift one up out of despair and, because of God's love, promise a better tomorrow. Whatever else we may have in life, if we have no hope we live in fear and wretchedness.

Many years ago I occasionally drove through the little town of Armstead, Montana. I have stopped there for a lunch break at a small cafe. But now the town is gone; it is at the bottom of a large reservoir created by the Clark Canyon Dam. High above the town that once was, people enjoy fishing and boating, often unaware that there was ever a town in that area.

After the decision was made to build the dam and long before the town was covered by water, it was interesting to observe what happened in the town. It simply died. No one painted a house or fixed a tumbled-down fence. No streets were repaired; no one bought property. No one planned for the future. The town did not drown when the water came to cover it. It had already died for want of hope. Any person, group, or society is doomed if it loses its hope. And we do well to remember that our ultimate hope is not in any human achievement, not in any political process, much as we must do our best in these human

FIREWEED AND ASHES   **17**

endeavors. Our reason for hope is in the very nature of God who loves the world and whose greatest power is manifest in life and growth, in the silent processes of the fireweed and the seeds—and not in the ashes.

Each year a day comes when I realize it is time again to write our Christmas letter—a letter in which we try to share a word of hope along with the family news. Generally this day comes not because of a date on the calendar, but because there is a morning, generally in late November, when I wake up to see that overnight the mountains have turned from green and brown to the white of winter snow. It is an awesome power that can silently, while the city sleeps, completely change our world as far as one can see, from the colors of autumn, from the blackened area where a summer range fire burned, to the clean fresh white of winter. It is an awesome silent power we celebrate at Christmas: a power that can change a world of despair into a world of hope. "For God so loved the world, that he [sent] his only begotten Son" to bring hope into the hearts of those who live in a troubled world. And He makes the fireweed bloom in the ashes of a devastated forest—fireweed that is a symbol of life and the forerunner of a new and productive forest.

In our celebration of this holy season, our family gatherings, our worship services, our giving and receiving, our reading again of the sacred story, our songs and our prayers, God is quietly planting seeds of hope and love, seeds that will grow even in the ashes of our human failures—seeds that will blossom into better understanding, more concern for each other, and a deeper appreciation for the gift of life in which we share together.

The message of Christmas is a word of hope. Bright

blossoms of fireweed speak of new life and new growth in the ashes of a burned-out forest or the rubble and destruction of a bombed city. There is a star in the sky on the darkest night. For unto us a child is born; the Word of our God becomes flesh and dwells among us. The Light shines in the darkness and the darkness can never overcome the light. That is God's way. The future is not in the ashes of the burned-out forest but in the restoring and healing power of new life—the blossoms and seeds of the fireweed. The future is not with the evil of Herod the king. The future is with the Child.

3

In All Generations

"Lord, thou hast been our dwelling place in all generations"
(Ps. 90:1).

When my mother died, after a long life that had given much to many people, I felt a keen sense of loss. For months I would find myself wanting to ask her about some event in our family history. Or I would reach for the phone to share with her some bit of good news or some plan that I was considering, only to be reminded that she would not be there to answer the phone and share in my interest. On the first Mother's Day after her death I found myself looking for a Mother's Day card before I realized I wouldn't need to send one. But with this sense of loss, there has also come some understanding and insight that has continued to grow—understanding that brings comfort and guidance.

As I sat in the church during the funeral service, there suddenly came to me the realization that I was now a part of the older generation. This was something quite new for me. A degree had been conferred upon me; I had graduated into a different level of life. The generation that had always been standing between me and eternity had moved up and on beyond the ticket counter or check-out stand, and there was no longer anyone standing between me and the great reality called *death* that is a part of life. When the angel appeared again and called, "Next please, just step this way," she would be opening the door for me. I could look back and see others in the line behind me, my children and my grandchildren, but now there was no one in front of me. It was something of a lonely feeling, but it also had about it a sense of importance. My new role carried honor and obligation; I wanted to accept it with pride and a determination to do well in it.

As a part of Mother's funeral service, a choir of fourteen of her grandchildren sang. As they sang I wondered: "Can Mother hear them now?" I had a very strong feeling that she did hear and that she smiled. For me the word *grandfather* took on a new and special meaning as I thought of my children's children. A favorite passage of Scripture came to mind with a new and deeper meaning: "Lord, thou has been our dwelling place in all generations."

In the years since my mother's death these great words from the ninetieth Psalm have continued to speak to me: "Before the mountains were brought forth, . . . from everlasting to everlasting, thou art God." They had very special meaning for me during a period when I was confused and troubled by an illness which truly frightened me and gave me many days of depression, a period which came and passed and from which I have recovered. These words reminded me that the God who had watched over Mother's childhood in Scotland, who had been with her as the orphan girl who came seeking her fortune in America, who had been with her in the trials and joys of raising a family, who had stood beside her at my father's grave and now had walked with her through the valley of

IN ALL GENERATIONS

the shadow and invited her into "the house of the Lord for ever"—this very God was with me. He was with my children and their children. He will be with them when, in their turn, they become the older generation, moving up in the line when my flight is called and I walk on through the gate—boarding pass ready—to fly through the friendly skies. It is a simple thought, yet in it there is acceptance, comfort, and assurance.

Mother, who gave me the bread of life literally and figuratively, has run the race ahead of me. In that relay race of the generations, she has handed me the baton and given me a good position on the track. It is no longer time for grief. It is time to accept with thankfulness the challenge to perform to the best of my ability that I might give to one who runs behind me a good position in the race and a keen awareness of the goal toward which we strive. The faith that was given to me, I have the privilege of giving to another. I have always been fascinated by great rivers that run down from the mountains to the sea, that continue to flow season after season, through flood times and periods of drought, and never run dry. Like the wonder of generations, there is no beginning and no ending but an endless stream that has its dwelling place in the eternal.

For many years I lived where I could see the south slope of the mountains that form the Continental Divide and the boundary between Idaho and Montana. These south slopes were the winter range for many elk that spent most of the summer in Montana and then migrated into Idaho for the winter because the south slopes had less timber and large open areas covered with grass and other forage plants.

Some years a sudden storm would bring deep snow a

little earlier than expected, and to get to their winter range the elk would have to travel for several miles through chest-deep snow and sometimes drifts that were even deeper. In order to get safely to their destination, the elk would string out single file, following one strong individual who would break through the drifts, take the brunt of the crusted snow, and make it much easier for those who followed in the well-defined trail made by the leader. By the time several elk had passed, a trench was cut through the snow as sharply as if it had been plowed by a snow plow. One could see these trails for miles, and I have even taken advantage of them when riding my horse in heavy snow.

When the snow was deep and drifts filled the gullies, no matter how strong the leader might be, soon or late, her strength would be used up. (An elk herd when traveling is led by a strong, mature female.) There would come a time when she would have to step aside, drop back, and let the next in line become the leader. But always the one who stepped aside, who had used up her strength in giving leadership, left behind a record of achievement and a path that made life better for those who followed her. Always through her wisdom and strength she had brought them closer to the mountain pastures that would be their hope and their sustenance through the difficult winter months that lay ahead. Through the cold and snow she had brought them closer to another springtime.

In the ultimate plans of a wise and loving God, we each find our place in the ever-moving line of generations. In our turn there comes a time to "break trail," our turn to buck the drifts and storms of life, knowing there are those who will follow and "break trail" in their genera-

IN ALL GENERATIONS

tion. When that time comes, when our strength fails and vision grows dim, it will be good to know that we can step aside, leaving a trail that others can safely follow: a path that is leading in the right direction so that the one who steps up to take our place will not have to backtrack and cast about for purpose and meaning. And we can step aside with confidence and assurance, knowing that the God who has guided us and been our "dwelling place" will just as surely be with those who follow. "Let thy work be manifest to thy servants,/and thy glorious power to their children" (Ps. 90:16, RSV).

4
Cabbages

All my life I have been blessed by a close association with gardens. Early childhood memories include picking and eating vine-ripened tomatoes, learning the difference between weeds and garden plants, proudly learning to use a hoe, "helping" my father select a ripe, sweet watermelon. In later years I have found that most parsonages have a yard large enough for a garden, even if a small one. Gardens have been an important source of our family's groceries.

Most of our gardens have included cabbage. We like cabbage, even boiled cabbage. It is very easy to grow, and it is good food. I have had the experience of growing cabbage where the wind blew and was constantly dumping a good deal of dirt and sand on everything. Once our garden was near an unpaved road with a good deal of traffic on it, and the supply of dirt and dust was almost constant all summer. But the remarkable cabbage can grow in a very dirty environment and still be perfectly clean inside. When I pick cabbages, I like to think about their ability to live clean lives in a dirty world and their gift of producing good food even in very unsavory circumstances.

The secret of the cabbage head is quite obvious. The cabbage grows from the inside out. It has a source of inner strength that can sustain it when outward conditions are bad. Because it is always growing from the inside, it stays clean even when things outside are dirty. This is a wonderful quality of character. I cannot imagine a cabbage, dirty on the inside and unfit to eat, giving as an excuse the fact that it was surrounded with dirty neighbors and had to live beside a dusty road. Cabbages can even be dusted on the outside with poison to kill the cabbage worms, and still, just inside the outer leaves, they are clean and pure.

Through the centuries this power of an "inner life" has given Christians the ability to live a good life in what is very often a bad world. No matter how filthy or corrupt the environment may be, the Christian who is growing spiritually from the inside has a source of strength that can keep the heart pure. Jesus said: "Blessed are the pure in heart: for they shall see God" (Matt. 5:8). He said it to people who lived in a city that had no sewage disposal system, a city where pollution was a terrible problem, and where morals were extremely low among a great many of the people—certainly among the Roman rulers and occupation forces. The psalmist, becoming acquainted with God, recognized this wonderful gift, saying: "Behold, thou desirest truth in the inward being;/therefore teach me wisdom in my secret heart" (Ps. 51:6, RSV).

Our real protection from the evil that surrounds us is the good within us. When we are under pressure, the only thing that can keep us from caving in is to be filled with something on the inside, so we can withstand the pressure from the outside.

I remember a frightening accident we had while pulling a horse trailer. The trailer separated from the pickup and rolled over several times. Very fortunately we were not carrying our horses, but the trailer was filled with as much baled hay as could possibly be packed in. The trailer was badly dented, but it was saved from being crushed by what was inside.

We all live in a world where we are surrounded with pressures that can crush us. There is crime, materialism, immorality of all sorts—one can make a long and pessimistic list. There is an ever-present fear that we have no future because of the atomic threat, so we compromise the present. These forces will cave us in unless we are filled from the inside with a greater force that can resist the pressure. The Christian faith provides this inner strength. Filled with power and joy and the goodness of God, we have an inner life that can produce abundance even in a far-from-perfect world. This is the good news that Christ came to proclaim.

At the end of his letter to the Philippians Paul put a very interesting postscript: "All the saints greet you, especially those of Caesar's household" (Phil. 4:22, RSV). The Christians in Caesar's household were servants and slaves for the most part. They were maintaining their Christian integrity while living right in the house of an emperor who was the very symbol of evil. Caesar's household has been associated with one of the most immoral, wicked, and evil places in history. Yet in the very midst of it were victorious Christians sending greetings and best wishes to other Christians.

CABBAGES

How could they do it? Like the lowly cabbage, they had an inner life that was a source of their life and growth. Growing from the inside, they were not shaped and flavored by the unwholesome elements in their environment. In the fourth chapter of Philippians we see the formula for this kind of living: "Whatever is true, whatever is honorable, whatever is just, whatever is pure, whatever is lovely, whatever is gracious, . . . if there is anything worthy of praise, think about these things" (Phil. 4:8, RSV). A life so filled has the power and inner resources to withstand the pressure of outside corruption.

A young man recently asked: "How can I stay clean in a dirty world?" It isn't easy. We certainly can't do it by avoiding all dirt. And we can't do it by cleaning up the world, much as we must continue to make our best efforts in this direction. If we try to live a real life in the real world, we will get the dirt dumped on us. The victory of Christian living that Paul knew so well and that Christian slaves in Caesar's household understood was the gaining, through spiritual resources and faith, of the ability to live a good life in a bad world—the ability to be involved in the worst if need be, get our hands dirty, and keep our minds clean. We can only do it by keeping close to Him who can "Create in me a clean heart, . . . and renew a right spirit within me" (Ps. 51:10).

Ships now sail the oceans in almost perfect safety. This has not been made possible by making oceans without storms and waves. It has been done by building ships that have the strength and ability to sail through storms. Because, in our modern world, we have accomplished some remarkable things in our standard of living in material ways—controlling diseases, producing good food and improved medicine—we are inclined to put too much emphasis on the outward circumstances of life. When these fail we may find we have nowhere to turn. It is important for us to remember that we still live in the same world in which the psalmist lived—we are still surrounded with much of the evil that was in Caesar's household. And we still have the sources of inner strength and life that sustained people of faith in those situations.

When I feel a bit discouraged about conditions in the world around me, it does me good to go into the garden and pick a nice head of cabbage. I may find it covered with grime and dust. Mud has been splashed on it by a heavy rain or the sprinkler. Several times it has been dusted with a poisonous compound to eliminate cabbage worms. But I know that because it grows from the inside, is constantly nourished by inner resources, and does not allow outer circumstances to pollute its inner character, I can take off just a few of the outer leaves and find a good, firm cabbage head that is clean, wholesome, and sweet.

5

Top for the Tree

A number of years ago I started quite a few young evergreen trees, some spruce and some pine. It has been a joy to watch them grow, and though we don't live now in the place where I started them, I still like to drive by from time to time and see how well they have developed. Evergreen trees such as the spruce and pine have their own definite shape if they have a chance to grow without restrictions, and it is much harder to shape them with pruning than it is fruit trees, oak, or maple. When they are broken by storms or accidents, it is harder to reshape them. These trees have a top branch that grows up and each year adds new height to the tree. I call it a leader. At the top is a bud from which several lateral branches grow and also the one that goes up and becomes the leader for the next year of growth. The regular annual growth and the natural symmetrical shape of the tree depends on the leader going straight up each year.

When one of our spruce trees was about eight feet high, something happened that destroyed the leader and tip. It may have been an accident or a strong wind that broke it off, or the bud may have been killed. Whatever happened, the leader did not reach up for the sun. The tree continued to grow out but not up; it was rapidly beginning to look like something other than a spruce tree. I would think that from the point of view of a spruce tree, this would be about the worst thing that could happen, a real catastrophe, something like a major life-changing accident or misfortune in the life of a person.

Not wanting to remove the tree from the row of trees it was in and not wanting it to grow into the shape of a round ball, I tried something that worked quite well. On the trunk of the tree I put a splint that would reach up past the top, took one of the lateral branches from below the leader, fastened it to the splint, pointed it toward the sky, and made a new top for the tree. This secondary branch became the leader. There will always be a bump in the trunk of the tree where the change took place, and it took a while for the tree to adjust. But through the wonderful powers of growth and adaption, the tree had new life and hope and is growing into quite a normal tree.

Pondering this life-giving ability to adjust, I realize we humans are much like the tree. We get hurt. We have major goals thwarted. It is important to remember that we do have secondary branches, and if we will accept help and be flexible, there is a source of power that can restore our life and hope and give new direction and a new top for our tree. I look back across the years and see how this process has meant much in my own life. When it seems that our dreams are stillborn and our best plans have not worked out, God is able to take some branch that we thought unimportant, some unused talent that we have neglected, and point it toward the sun, giving us new direction in place of defeat and despair.

TOP FOR THE TREE

I started high school in 1932 and carried with me dreams of a college education and an interesting and worthwhile career. High on my list was my desire to work with nature in forestry or wildlife management. I was active in a church youth group and thought some about being a minister, and I gave some thought to being a doctor. But my high school years were the worst years of the Great Depression. We were not making money on our farm; one summer no money at all passed through our family, yet we were fortunate to have food and shelter. But the dream of college grew dimmer as graduation grew nearer.

During my senior year I heard that the Methodist Church was trying to keep a dying college alive. It was not too far from where I lived. I could hitchhike the distance in a day or less. Work scholarships were offered students; faculty worked for room and board and promises. One of my high school teachers was moving there to teach and encouraged me to go with him. I did. It was a good year of working with wonderful dedicated people, but the school had to face reality and closed. It seemed the top was blown out of my career tree.

However, things were not hopeless. With a friend from our church youth group I found that Willamette University in Salem, Oregon, another Methodist school, would accept our freshman year credits, so we decided to take our chances and migrate to Salem. There I got a job in a boardinghouse, met a tree surgeon with whom I apprenticed, and found I had some skill with a pruning saw and was a natural-born tree climber. With a pay-as-you-go plan, I was able to stay in school. A wonderful professor took an interest in me; he encouraged me to major in sociology and prepare for a career in teaching. I began to see myself with an interesting academic life and the role of a college professor. A fine new top was beginning to take shape in my dream tree.

During my senior year my major professor arranged a scholarship for me at a graduate school, but by the time I entered the school the dark clouds of World War II were rolling in. I became involved with a group of Quakers who were helping refugees from Hitler's Germany. For me the quiet, appealing academic life of a professor seemed suddenly to be blown away.

Again my thoughts turned to the ministry, and I found a secondary branch was being made into a new top for the tree. I transferred to a Methodist seminary and was given the opportunity to pastor a small church while I attended seminary. Now looking back over the past forty years, I can see how God was able to take a branch of my life that I had considered a secondary branch, direct it upward to become the leading branch of my life, and give my life a shape and direction that I had never thought possible. I am thankful for that.

We live in a world in which there is always a great deal of change. Sometimes the storms are violent like wars and depressions. We get battered and broken. There are changes in the concept of the family. Economic patterns are very insecure. Some people are changing jobs because they want to; great numbers are being rudely pushed out of chosen work because of changing technology and world markets. Many of the people I know best, the farmers and ranchers, are facing a critical time of change in their industry and way of life. Tree tops are being broken.

In such a time, whether we face a job loss, a failing

business, a broken home, or some other crisis, we can always trust that God has a plan for us. He does not make "one-talent" people. There are other branches in our lives that can be pointed toward the sun when the cherished top is blown out of our tree.

God can reshape our lives when they are damaged. Ours is the God who took Moses who was running from a murder charge in Egypt, who considered himself unfit for leadership because of a speech problem, and made him the leader of his people and the great liberator (Ex. 2:11; 3:6). He took the hot-tempered Peter whose life plans were crushed by the horror of the crucifixion, who was so broken and afraid that he denied having ever known Jesus, and made him a courageous leader of the early church. One of the greatest reshaping jobs of all time was the making of the apostle Paul from the hate-filled persecutor of the church, Saul of Tarsus. Surely if God can reshape lives like these He can handle any situation that we will put into his care. There is no limit to God's ability to bring about new life and to redirect that which is bent or broken.

It is possible to start a poplar tree just by sticking a fresh-cut branch in the ground. I started a number in that fashion at one time, and after the first year of growth, several of them were broken off completely by being stepped on by cows. Because they had taken root, the next year each of the broken ones put out a whole new little tree that in a few years was almost as tall and straight as if it had never been destroyed.

I never cease to marvel at God's ability to restore and redirect whether it be in the life of a tree or a person. Sometimes His doing is beyond our understanding, and to us it seems a miracle. Isaiah uses an image that has always fascinated me. He speaks of God's action as a "root [growing] out of a dry ground" (53:2). That is where I would least expect a root to sprout and grow. I would expect it to require moist ground at least. But God's ways are not always our ways. And I have learned without any doubt that He can give a new top to a tree.

6

Pruning Peach Trees

"Every branch that does bear fruit he prunes, that it may bear more fruit" (John 15:2, RSV).

During the years that I attended college I earned a large part of my living with a pruning saw. That experience has given me a great appreciation for the Christian symbol of the vine and the branches. My work was with trees and apples more than with vines and grapes, but the symbolism is certainly the same. Unfruitful branches have to go, and branches that are disconnected from their source of life and strength cannot be fruitful. But my favorite part of the Scripture passage about the vine and branches is the line that speaks of the fruitful branch that still needs pruning, so it "may bear more fruit." For the Christian, there is always the desire and opportunity to improve one's relationship with the Source of our life and strength and to become more productive.

There are three purposes in pruning trees. Much of the work we do is to make a tree look better. That's good! A major purpose of a tree is to add beauty to the world. I call this ornamental or cosmetic pruning. The object is to make the tree look like that kind of tree should look—to bring out its true character. If you have seen a maple tree that was pruned primarily to keep the branches from interfering with power wires, you may have seen a maple tree that looked more like a cactus than a maple. Sometimes this has to be done, but in a world that needs all the beauty it can find, there is always something very sad about it. When we start to prune a maple or a walnut or an oak, we have in mind an artist's image of that kind of tree, and we do our best to help it conform to that ideal image. As it conforms to its ideal image, the tree also gains structural strength. The unpruned and undirected tree is more easily broken by the wind. I think that in the mind of God, who is the pruner of persons, there must be for each of us an ideal image toward which He would have us grow.

Another purpose of pruning, which applies only to fruit trees, is for maximum production, both in quantity and quality of fruit. The well-pruned branch is open to the sunlight, is not broken down by a large number of small and undesirable fruits, and is limited so as to be within reach of one who comes to gather the fruit at harvesttime. The wise orchardist knows there is little value in the high and wandering branch that bears fruit out of reach of anyone but the birds.

A third purpose of pruning, one I have reflected on a great deal as a pastor, I call reconstructive pruning. This is the kind that one is called on most to do on fine old ornamental trees. It is the work we do when trees have suffered injury generally after a heavy snowfall or a high wind.

Some years ago I started some peach trees by the house where we lived. I had high hopes for the trees and wanted them to grow into fine productive trees. I knew I had to

PRUNING PEACH TREES

direct and guide their growth; to simply ignore them and let them grow in tangled and undisciplined ways would certainly not be an indication of my care for them, and I trust that is how God feels about me. Because they were my trees and I was truly fond of them, I used my pruning saw and shears. When I cut off unproductive and dead branches and piled them to be burned, I was not angry with them. I did not burn them to punish them. I did so simply to make the tree more fruitful, strong, and attractive.

Sometimes branches get wild notions and try to be the tallest, longest branches on the tree. These have to be eliminated or cut down to size, and I suspect that sometimes the Great Gardener has to cut us down to size when we have been growing in the wrong direction or have wrong aims such as being the tallest branch, regardless of how much fruit we bear. There are times when I think I have felt God's pruning shears, and I have not always appreciated it. But I believe God has been trying to do for me what I tried to do for my peach trees, not trying to hurt, or punish, but trying to redirect and reshape, making me more productive and more able to relate to the life-giving strength of the tree.

Those of us who have weathered some storms in life know the importance of reconstructive pruning. One young peach tree, heavily weighted with green fruit, was struck with an unusual wind gust that not only tore off a large branch but took it off clear back to the tree, tearing out a large section of the tree trunk itself. Because I knew this was a good quality tree I began reconstructive pruning.

That little peach tree was so badly torn apart that it

was hardly recognizable as a peach tree. But with reconstructive pruning, over a period of years it was restored not only to production but to a fairly good appearance. Because it was so badly torn on one side, one of my first efforts was to restore balance and symmetry. I had to begin by cutting off good branches on the side not torn—that was the only way I could restore balance and allow it to grow again into the shape it was intended to have. I'm sure this put limitations on the tree, and I suppose if it could talk it might have complained and asked: "Why are these limitations being imposed on me?" Sometimes when God does reconstructive pruning on us, we have these same feelings and this same question. It is sometimes hard for us to see that present hurts and limitations may be helping us to develop strength and character in years to come. The gardener with the pruning saw can always see farther ahead than can the tree.

The world in which we live, with all its storms and adversity, gives to all of us some terrible hurts at times. There are often wind gusts that we have no way of predicting. Sometimes branches are torn off; sometimes it seems our very being is torn apart. I think at such times God is there to begin His reconstructive pruning. And sometimes, when it seems the pruning is severe, it is because He doesn't want us to heal in a lopsided way. He wants to make room for new branches to grow, branches that may add dimensions to our lives that we never dreamed we had. And if we are peach trees, He wants us to regain our characters as peach trees rather than letting us grow misshapen as storm-torn wild junipers.

And we must wait. God's schedule is often very different from ours. One of the greatest lessons I have learned

PRUNING PEACH TREES

from pruning trees: I can cut away that which hinders healing and may cause deformity. I can take away that which should be removed. But only a power much greater than mine can bring the new growth, restore the structure, and bring the new life. For this I generally have to wait at least a year and often more than that. When I am impatient and find myself trying to hurry God, I like to remember my own best efforts pruning peach trees.

7

Prayer on the Run

Years ago when I was doing some ranching with the help of my children, we had some exciting moments. The calves were born in late winter or early spring when the weather could turn very cold. Sometimes a newborn calf would be so cold and weak that it could not nurse without help. Sometimes the new mother would be confused and move about and make it difficult for the calf. And it was imperative that the calf receive nourishment right away if it was to overcome the cold and survive. Also, the nursing is important in establishing a bond between the calf and the mother, so the mother will properly care for the calf.

This situation meant that the cow had to be brought in, restrained, milked by hand if her udder was too distended and sensitive, and the calf often had to be given some guidance and support in its first awkward efforts to find a teat and get the action started. Our cows were not exceptionally wild or mean, but they were range cattle, and they were not accustomed to confinement or restraint. Our ranch operation was small and new, and we did not

PRAYER ON THE RUN

have the most sophisticated methods for handling cattle. We had a good round corral with a snubbing post in the center, and a high fence had been built for catching and training range-raised horses.

When we needed to work with a cow, we would bring her into the corral, rope her by the head and one front foot, and snub her to the snubbing post. With her snubbed tight and standing on three legs, we generally could handle things quite well and get the new calf a tummy full of milk and a general grasp of how to proceed on his own. Our problem came in releasing the cow.

It was not possible to explain to the cow that we were doing all these things for the benefit of her and her calf; by the time we were finished, the cow would be extremely resentful, sometimes to the extent of an unreasoning rage that was ready to vent itself on anything or anyone. Cows have a natural instinct to become very anxious and upset when they are separated from the herd which is a source of security. This is greatly increased by the instinct to protect their calves. Getting a rope off a really angry cow can be a lot harder than putting it on.

The loop in a lariat is made by the rope running through a very small loop built into the end which is called, in ranch language, the hondu. To solve the problem of releasing an angry cow, snubbed with a very tight rope, I used a breakaway hondu. It is made of metal with a release mechanism. One can simply jerk a short leather thong that will open the hondu and give an instant release, no matter how tight the rope may be.

The kids and I had a team system worked out for releasing angry cows, and it worked very well. I would be holding the snubbing rope with a couple of hitches around the post in the center of the corral. One of the kids would get up next to the cow, get hold of the leather thong on the hondu, and give it a jerk. The instant it released, we would sprint for the fence and climb it. When the cow gave her first attention to her calf, there was no problem.

But quite often she would give her first attention to destroying her tormentors. One could sometimes tell by her tone of voice what her intention was. There is an indescribable bawl that a cow makes when she has murder on her mind. But we had a very strict rule: we were to climb the fence first and check on the cow's intentions second. With about twenty feet to go to get to the fence, there was not time to stop to see if the cow was after us. A thousand pounds of very angry beef can be intimidating, and when one could feel and hear for sure that she was right behind, one was inclined to say a short prayer.

This moment of prayer was not a time to kneel quietly. It wasn't even a time to bow our heads or fold our hands. Our heads had to be up, our eyes open, and our hands extended reaching for the top rail on the fence. With a very agile and angry cow, there were times when we made the top rail, looked right down into that cow's wild-looking eyes, felt her hot breath on our feet and concluded our brief prayer with "Thank God, we made it."

Prayer in this setting may seem to some to be a bit profane, but really it isn't. Surely one's prayer life should not be limited to such situations, but for the really active person, prayer on the run is a very natural and almost instinctive response to something in life that is greater than we are. These spontaneous and very sincere prayers are often more realistic and honest than some that are more carefully planned. I like to define prayer as our

PRAYER ON THE RUN

awareness of God, our recognition of His place in our lives, and our response to communication with Him. It is unfortunate if we fail to recognize these prayers on the run as being true prayers, which I think they are.

One of my heroes is Robert E. Lee. I think he was one of the greatest generals this country ever produced. He went through some terrible heartbreak in a cause he could not win, but he was a man of prayer. Lee refers in his writing to what he called his "prayers on horseback," and certainly the circumstances under which he prayed were such that one didn't have a chance to get off the horse to pray. These prayers were sincere. They were from the depth of his being. They dealt with his deepest concerns and needs. And I think that most of us will find, if we honestly reflect on our lives, that some of our most sincere and meaningful prayers have been spontaneous and, in a true sense, prayers on the run. The psalmist must have thought of this when he wrote: "Where can I go from your Spirit? You know everything about me. You search my path, my lying down, and my getting up. Wherever I go, Your right hand shall lead me" (author's version of Ps. 139:1-10).

It is not good to separate our prayers from our actions. When we are running fast, it is important to remember that God is running with us. Life can be a pretty lonely business. Sometimes we are not only running, but we are running scared. It is a good day when we come to know that we don't have to go back to home base to check in with God. We will never run so fast that we leave Him, and wherever we are running, He will be there to meet us when we get there.

There is a deep mystery about prayer. When we really

think hard about it, most of us have some doubts. In fact, it is when we think hard about it that the doubt creeps in. It is almost impossible to have a really meaningful prayer in a religion class while studying the nature and meaning of prayer. But when your small plane is running low on fuel in a fog, when your child is undergoing critical surgery, or when in thankfulness you face the greatest opportunity of your life, there is something so natural and real about your prayer that doubt has no place to linger.

A favorite story from my childhood is about Grandfather's beard. It was a long and full beard in which he took pride. One night as he held his granddaughter on his lap she asked: "When you sleep, do you put your beard under the covers or on top of the covers?" He realized he didn't know, so that night when he went to bed, Grandfather worked on the problem. He put his beard under the covers, and that didn't seem right. He kept it above the covers, and that was awkward. It troubled him so that he couldn't sleep, and finally he got up and cut off his beard.

A close personal relationship is to be lived more than studied, whether it be the bond of love in our marriage or the bond of trust between us and our God. We can be so philosophical about a relationship that we tend to destroy its intimate and functional quality.

When our youngest daughter was about ten, she was just learning to swim. None of us are good swimmers. I have learned to swim enough for survival purposes. Our daughter was eager to show me how well she could swim. We had a small artificial lake on the ranch, and we went out on a raft about fifty yards from shore. I took an inner tube attached to a long rope, thinking if she had a prob-

PRAYER ON THE RUN

lem I could throw it to her. She asked me to throw out the inner tube, and she would swim out to it. I did, and she started to swim. But being clumsy in the water, each time she reached for the tube, instead of getting a hold on it she just bumped it away from her.

The water was very clear, and I suddenly realized that she was swimming but under the surface. I went in after her. When I got her head above water and started for shore, I remembered that I am not a very good swimmer. I'm glad she didn't know what a poor swimmer I am because her complete trust made things easier. When I asked her to just hang on and keep low in the water, she did. I asked God to help me get to shore. There was nothing sophisticated about this, and I never had time or energy to wonder about whether or not God answers prayers. When we got to shore, I said: "Thank God we made it."

These were very sincere prayers. There was nothing put on about this because I really needed help to swim better than I thought I could. She never saw it all as much of a problem. She got into deep water, and Dad pulled her out—that's what dads are for. And I think that deep down in every person, there is an instinct for God as natural as that little girl's natural confidence and trust in a father that she reached out to and took hold of that day in the water. In our prayers under pressure it just pops out, even if we don't say much about it at other times.

People who do not consider themselves the least bit religious will almost automatically make a little prayer of thanksgiving when danger passes, and tension is relieved. Thank God we found him. Thank God he came through the crash alive. We are made in such a way that we have to have someone to thank, and God is the one who is there to thank and praise. When I was a child and something wonderful happened at school, I just couldn't run home fast enough to tell my mother about it. I find that all through life I've been making the same childlike short reports to God.

Prayers of reflection are important and help our spirits grow. But sometimes we judge ourselves harshly and think we are not practicing Christians because our prayers are not as formal as we think they should be. We need to remember that our prayers while we run are very real and important. They say something good about our relationship with God. And even if we are running faster than we like, and even if we are terribly out of breath, no matter how fast we run we are never out of the hearing of God who is running with us step for step.

8

When the Rocks Talk

The world of nature is filled with an honesty and integrity that can be an inspiration. Only human beings indulge in useless and dishonest speech. It is refreshing to spend some time working with animals or plants because genuine love and truthful speech are so important in our human relationships. Surely this is the appeal we find in growing a garden, having a pet, and spending time in a park. I am sure that experience in the world of nature can help us enrich our lives in a world of people. Nature is not always kind, but it is always truthful. There is never a time when one can feel more lonely than when surrounded by people who never let you know how they really feel about you or anything that is of real importance.

Jesus once said that if He didn't speak out on a theme the very rocks would cry out (Luke 19:40). The first time I read that I thought it impossible. Rocks don't talk. Then for a while I worked in a mine, and I found that rocks do talk, and when the rocks talk one had better listen. There is no put on, no pretending when the rocks talk. It means they are moving. It means there is some readjustment going on, probably as a result of mining activity, and one had better take appropriate action. When rocks talk and say to get out fast, there is no faking, no pretense. I have heard the rocks talk, and I have never stopped to argue because they always mean what they say.

Most of my life I have enjoyed working with animals, and I've learned to pay attention to what they say. They don't talk with words like people do, and sometimes they've been called dumb animals, but I prefer to call them quiet animals. Sometimes the word *dumb* is misconstrued. Animals can teach us a great deal about honest communication.

In my work with animals there have been orphaned lambs, pigs to feed, cows to milk, and a number of dogs and cats. When I was eight years old I began driving a team of horses at haying time. As I have tried to communicate with various animals I have been impressed by their integrity. I have never had an animal that tried to pretend, put on airs, or seek to mislead me in order to make himself appear to be greater or wiser; I have never known an animal to pretend a false humility. In play, a dog will seem to be a show-off, but there is always a forthright and childlike honesty about it. When an animal likes you and enjoys your company, the message comes through loud and clear, and it is never said just to be polite or proper. You also get a clear statement when the animal is disgusted with you and prefers to be left alone.

I have worked more with horses than with any other animals, and I have never known a horse to give a false communication. When a well-trained horse thinks you ought to be kicked, he may be too well trained to kick

WHEN THE ROCKS TALK

you, but he is not giving you indications that he likes you. His displeasure is very evident. And if he likes you and nuzzles you he means it, and he is not doing it just to get you in position to bite you or walk on you. If a horse decides you ought to be kicked, he will always give it his best shot. He will try to kick you as hard and as sincerely as he can. There is no play acting, no shadow boxing like one gets from some people. When my horse gives me a little chuckle, a little nicker of appreciation, it is always genuine, and many times I have heard this and wished that I could be as sure about the remarks of some people who have made polite appreciative sounds.

Twice in my life I have had a horse tell me in no uncertain terms that I was being inconsiderate, too hasty, and expecting too much. In these instances when I failed to pay attention or chose to ignore what I was being told, I paid a price—once a cracked rib and another time a bruised thigh muscle with a neatly printed purple horseshoe on it. This same consistent honesty can be seen in the communication between animals. Deliberate misrepresentation is not practiced.

This basic honesty seems to be a natural law of survival and one that people may be treating too lightly in our "civilized" society. Nothing hurts relationships and creates isolation and despair more than deceit. And nothing builds trust and friendship more than sincere speech that opens our hearts to one another. In a crowded world where loneliness is a major problem I need to ask how long it has been since I said anything that really helped anyone and gave encouragement, cheered someone who was depressed, or simply indicated that I cared and could share my feelings. In 2 Corinthians 1, verse 6, Paul spoke of the need for genuine love and truthful speech. They go hand in hand. Communication in nature is naturally honest, and our human problem is our tendency to be artificial.

When your cat is purring, things are all right: she is not faking or putting you on. She is contented and quite willing to share that information. When that cat is growling and claws are extended beyond the paws, she is not fooling, and one will do well to believe what she is saying.

It is a joy to listen to a mother grouse or pheasant talking to her little ones. Her little clucking sound is saying: "Hey kids, here is something good to eat." Then quite a different sound. She has discovered that she is being watched. She says: "Hide quickly, and don't come out until I call you." She is never bluffing, never pretending, and the children listen with respect. One reason there are no juvenile delinquents among pheasants or grouse or deer or elk or bears is that when Mama speaks, she is always sincere and has in mind that which is best for her children. There is never a promise that is not kept if there is any possible way to keep it.

I have enjoyed stalking antelope just to see how close I could get to a group without them running away. I remember a group that were in a little valley where I had excellent cover, and the wind was right for me. I got within twenty-five yards of them. Across from me on a ridge was an old doe, the sentinel. She knew I was there, but she could not be sure what I was. Trusting her, the rest of the antelope were feeding peacefully. When I got close enough to pose real danger had I been a bobcat or coyote, she stamped her foot and gave a signal. Every

WHEN THE ROCKS TALK

head came up; every animal paid attention. Not one of them took the attitude that she was fooling them. Not one of them thought her a show-off, just trying to show herself the best foot stamper in the crowd. They knew her speech was genuine, her concern for them sincere. When she wheeled to run, everyone in the group was with her. They knew she would never give a false impression just to improve her own self-image.

So often in things that mean the most, we humans communicate the least. We become evasive or try to pretend for the sake of keeping up appearances. I need to ask: How long since I have talked to anyone about prayer, eternal life, how to deal with death, or personal goals for life—things that really make a difference? And has my communication been with genuine love and truthful speech? Perhaps you have a loved one or a friend who is being stalked by loneliness or fear of illness or a lack of faith, and you have not done even as much as the old antelope lookout to share your knowledge and concern.

When the rocks talk, they mean it; when the quiet creatures of earth—the animals and birds—speak, they mean it and are honest in their speech. We could do well to study their wisdom and copy their ways. We will do well to remember the wise words of the apostle Paul as he spoke to the church at Corinth. He knew the importance of sincere communication, genuine love, and truthful speech. He said: "Our mouth is open to you, Corinthians; our heart is wide" (2 Cor. 6:11).

9

Square Watermelons

> *"Don't let the world around you squeeze you into its own mould" (Rom. 12:2, Phillips).*

When I was a child I enjoyed helping my mother make butter at home with an old-fashioned churn. It was great fun: put the cream in the churn, work the plunger up and down for a while, and soon there were gobs of butter floating around in buttermilk. I used to think it was some kind of miracle—maybe it was. We took the butter, and, after working the excess moisture out of it, we squashed it down into little oblong boxes. We smoothed it off even, turned it out, and each block of butter was exactly the right shape, weighed exactly a pound, and was very lacking in character. Whenever I read the twelfth chapter of Romans I can see those butter molds and almost feel the world trying to squeeze me into one of them. I'm glad Paul has warned us against this and shown us ways in which God can shape us to the pattern that He has in mind for us—the pattern that can be our own special and unique personality. God has in mind for each of us an original pattern; He is not interested in standard models.

Some years ago in the *Upper Room* daily devotional magazine, there was a story about a project to grow square watermelons. They were to have great advantages in shipping and storing and would stack up much better in the store than the rounded, odd-shaped ordinary melons. The plan called for a box around each little melon as it grew, causing it to conform to the shape of the box. Having observed melons and squash in my own garden, I think this might work. I have seen them grow, crowded against a board fence or a rock, into odd patterns. But the account did point out that one should not save seeds from a square watermelon in expectation of growing more of them. Even if you grow a square watermelon by forcing it to conform to a set pattern, God has put a life force in the seeds that will make every effort to grow a round or oblong melon if it gets a chance.

Growing square watermelons is a very artificial business. I'm sure the apostle Paul observed that too many people are willing to be artificial in their attempt to fit some pattern just because "everyone seems to be doing it." We might find that we "stack up" nicely, but to what purpose? I once had some melons to sell, and I admit it was a problem to pile them up and to keep them from rolling around and getting broken. But there was something nice about every melon being just a little different, and it was fun to watch the customers trying to pick out the ones they wanted. One can't do that with nice neat two-quart cartons of milk. I like buying watermelons— there is always an element of adventure in it.

Horses have always been an enjoyable part of my adult life. For many years I served in rural churches where I could enjoy riding in connection with ranching and big-game hunting. After moving to a church in Boise, Idaho, and away from a ranching area, I became involved in endurance riding. It is a great sport though relatively unknown because it has very little appeal to spectators. We ride the horses that are the marathon runners of the horse world. The typical ride is fifty to one hundred miles, often through scenic, unpopulated country on back roads and forest trails. The ride is actually a race, the fastest time wins, but it is under strict rules, carefully controlled conditions, with judges who are veterinarians so that horses are not overridden and injured. Riders are very considerate of their horses. One rides to win, but one also wants to ride again next week, and in most cases the rider is the owner of the horse. The horse and rider are a team, working together. Endurance horses don't start till they are five, and many are still doing well into their late teens.

One of the hazards of a ride is losing time because of getting lost. The sponsor of the ride marks the trail, generally by flagging it with bright-colored surveyor's tape. On a fifty-mile ride, as the horses get spaced out at their various speeds, one often finds himself riding alone unless a definite plan has been made to ride with someone who rides at about the same pace.

But riding alone is not a primary cause of getting lost. The most common causes of getting lost come from the tendency to ride in relation to other riders and failing to keep close attention on the trail markers. Two or more riders trotting along together will be visiting with each other and miss a trail marker. Or even more likely to miss the trail is the rider who is following and possibly trying to catch a rider up ahead who has already missed the trail.

Or, when one is riding alone, there is the danger of

SQUARE WATERMELONS

following the tracks of the other riders rather than the trail markers. It is always embarrassing to catch the rider ahead only when that rider turns around and starts back, realizing he has missed the trail and is off the course. Often on soft ground the trail is well marked by tracks of leading horses as well as by trail markers. But this can also lead to trouble, and when tracks disagree with the trail marker, one follows the marker and wishes the best of luck to the riders who made the tracks.

And the trails are not exclusive. In some areas one may hit tracks made by some rider who is not even involved in the contest. On a recent ride in southwest Idaho, I was watching tracks and trail markers and noticed tracks that suddenly left the route of the ride. I took a second look and saw they were made by horses that were not wearing shoes. Our route was across a range that is also used by several bands of wild horses. What a ride I might have had following those tracks! One can surely blow a good day's riding just by riding hard to catch another fast horse that has already gone astray.

One reason we all like the story of David and Goliath is because David, the shepherd boy, had faith in the Lord's ability to guide him and the courage to do his own thing. When David volunteered to fight the giant Goliath, King Saul was naturally pleased and insisted that David wear the king's armor and fight with the king's sword. It must have been flattering to the young man. In deference to his king, David tried on the armor. I suspect he had never worn armor before. He could hardly walk in it, let alone freely and accurately swing his slingshot arm. I imagine he felt worse than I did on my first pair of snowshoes. But David had killed lions and bears with his slingshot. He knew what he could do with that. He politely declined to wear the king's armor, honor though it was. David said to Saul, " 'I cannot go with these; for I am not used to them.' And David put them off" (1 Sam. 17:39).

So David took his slingshot and the skill that was his special gift, and we know the rest of the story. If he had tried to be a square watermelon by wearing the king's armor and getting pressed into the mold that was the pattern for the fighting man of his time, David would have been killed as a young man.

Paul warned us against conformity, against being pressed into the mold of the world, and he gave us very good suggestions to help us avoid this. He said we are to present our bodies as living sacrifices; we must realize that what we have has been entrusted to us by God and take care of it as belonging to God. I once needed a cattle truck to haul a load of cattle to a sale, and a friend graciously offered me the use of his truck. It was a fine new truck. I remember how carefully I drove it—better than if it had been my own. I certainly didn't want to return to such a gracious friend a truck that was dented and banged up. Surely God who has graciously loaned me my earthly physical equipment deserves to have it cared for in the best possible manner. Then Paul said to be transformed by the renewing of the mind. What a wonder and marvel is the mind. It can make us or break us. And the Christian has the promise of having that mind that was in Christ Jesus our Lord (Phil. 2:5). That is how we can escape the big squeeze. Paul said to think with sober judgment. Don't cherish exaggerated ideas of yourself (Rom. 12:3). Don't be too concerned about taking credit.

At the time of year when the geese are flying south, I

SQUARE WATERMELONS

am always reminded of the wonderful fable by Aesop. There is a little turtle who feels so sad because he can't fly south with the geese. He has lived all summer in a pond with his friends the geese and doesn't want to be left behind. He gets a great idea. He finds a stick, goes to a couple of geese, and asks them to carry him south on the stick. If a goose will take each end of the stick in its beak, the turtle will take hold of the middle with his mouth, and he will be carried south. The geese agree. The idea works just fine. They are flying along at a high altitude when someone sees them and says, "That is certainly a brilliant idea. I wonder who thought of that?" The turtle cannot resist opening his mouth to say: "It was my idea." And that is the end of the fable and the turtle.

We are reminded that "through the grace of God we have different gifts" (Rom. 12:6, Phillips). We are urged to use them, for surely as we use our unique gifts we avoid being squeezed into a mold. And as we "have no imitation Christian love. . . . Let us have real warm affection for one another" (Rom. 12:9, Phillips). Then we have a dependable guide to developing our own style of relating to others. When pressured by the big squeeze of conformity, we can ask the question, who do I really love, and what does my love do for the person or persons I love? What does it do to my relationship with God? Because it is genuine it is dependable. As Paul pointed out in another famous passage, many things pass away, but "love knows no limit to its endurance" (1 Cor. 13:8, Phillips). It is, in fact, the one thing that still stands when all else has fallen.

I think that when we come to the end of the day, those whom we have loved deeply will mean more to us than that which we have accomplished in material ways. Some of the most unhappy people have been admired by many but loved by no one. They have accomplished much but loved little. The world will press you into its mold if it can, but you don't need to be a square watermelon even if they stack up better. You can be yourself as God intended you to be, using the formula He has given us. If your best talent is with a slingshot, use it, and use it well and proudly. Don't try to wear the king's armor or use the king's sword even if it might be considered quite an honor.

10

Every Valley Lifted Up

"Every valley shall be lifted up, and every mountain and hill be made low" (Isa. 40:4, RSV).

The sport of endurance riding that involves cross-country horseback rides of fifty miles or more has taken me to many interesting places and introduced me to vast areas of scenery that one never sees from major highways. On the way to a ride in the Danskin Mountains north of Mountain Home, Idaho, I saw the road I was traveling appear to go almost straight up. Driving my van, which does not have four-wheel drive, and pulling my horse trailer, I had the feeling that I would never be able to drive up that road. I was crossing the north side of the Snake River plain which rises very gently toward the hills. As the road reached the edge of the plain and started up toward the hills, it went straight ahead up onto a bench land that is the beginning of the mountains. The road went straight, with no curve to give depth perception. As it started up onto the bench land at a much steeper grade than on the plain, there was no way to see, from a few miles back, that it did have a reasonable grade. It appeared to be impossible.

There is an element of faith involved in approaching a

road of this kind. I'm sure most of us who travel have seen this phenomenon to some extent on many highways where the lack of depth perception makes the road appear impossibly steep. So I approached that road believing it wasn't as steep as it looked from a distance. Someone before me must have traveled that way, or there wouldn't be a road. I continued on, as my map indicated I should; as I got closer to the hill and actually began to climb, I could see it from a better angle. I was able to drive up it and found it difficult but not impossible as it had appeared. I would have missed a great day of riding if I had given up on that road on the basis of its appearance from about five miles back on the plain. Confidence in the builders of roads helped me continue in the face of what appeared too difficult. And in the ups and downs of life, a confidence in God's guidance and mercy can save us from despair. It can keep us from climbing mountains before we get to them or giving up because dark valleys seem to be the end of the world.

It was probably after a hard day of working his way through the hills on a pretty tough path that Isaiah, remembering his faith, declared: "Every valley shall be lifted up,/and every mountain and hill be made low;/the uneven ground shall become level,/and the rough places a plain" (RSV).

This is a great word of comfort for those of us who are simply having a rough time from day to day. Maybe we don't have any great ridges to cross or deep canyons to get through. Maybe our problem is that we have to work with some very abrasive people; maybe it is a collection of rocks on the path, and we are constantly stubbing our toes. The road grader of faith helps us see things as they

EVERY VALLEY LIFTED UP

really are and not as they appear through the eyes of fear and the feelings of panic.

One of the great joys of a vacation is the time spent traveling the great freeways of our country, noting the cuts and fills, the places where valleys have been literally lifted up, and mountains brought low, so that we ride smoothly along on "rough places" that have been made a plain, and one remembers he is never on vacation from the goodness of God.

One day I visited a large ranch looking for the rancher. I saw his young son sitting on the corral fence, and we visited. We talked about the size and beauty of the ranch in its mountain surroundings, and the little boy, with an expression of pride on his face, swung his hand to indicate the whole hemisphere and said: "You know, my daddy owns it all!" I'm sure this belief gave the boy a wonderful sense of security and belonging. When I am out in the hills or traveling across the vast expanse of the skies and looking down from a jetliner, or looking at a field ready for harvest, I feel like that little boy. I like to remember that my Father owns it all. It reminds me that I am someone, and I'm not having to go it alone.

Almost anywhere we go we can be constantly reminded of God's power and goodness. Roads and highways do this in a remarkable way, and sometimes it seems that Isaiah was able to foresee a modern highway. When we travel, we don't have to descend into every gully or climb to the top of every ridge. The valley has been lifted up, and the mountain brought low. When Isaiah traveled, he walked or rode a donkey, and no one had gone ahead to prepare a well-graded and smooth road. He would have loved the roads we already have. To him every high place was a difficult barrier that had to be painfully climbed, and every valley or canyon or ravine was a hazard where he had to climb down and then back up. There were always rocks which hurt one's feet or caused one to stumble. In some places he had to work hard to make as much as ten miles in a day. So in his dreams and visions he likened God's care to a road that was made smooth and a way in the wilderness made straight and safe. Remembering Isaiah's vision, we can see in these blessings a wonderful symbol for our faith.

Often as I have traveled a freeway I have wished I could have Isaiah with me. Imagine his amazement as he travels through a great cut in the mountain and across a deep ravine that has been filled or bridged, where one doesn't even have to slow down. Imagine his wonder when he sees how nearly he visualized this very road so long before it was constructed. He would enjoy seeing some construction in progress, seeing the great earth-moving machines as they level the high places, fill up the low areas, and make straight the difficult curves. Isaiah would likely exclaim: "The glory of the Lord shall be revealed,/and all flesh shall see it together,/for the mouth of the Lord has spoken" (Isa. 40:5, RSV). It would be great fun to drive across the country today with Isaiah and hear him exclaim: "That's just what I dreamed of when I was trying to get through those hills back in Palestine."

As I drive the highways today I remember that only two generations ago, my own grandparents struggled up and down these hills in wagons and must have also dreamed of a day when the "rough places" could be made plain. A modern highway is a great symbol of God's action in our lives. One of the most-feared valleys that He

EVERY VALLEY LIFTED UP

lifts up is the valley of the shadow of death. He has lifted it up through our knowledge of the resurrection—taken away our fear of that dark and deep valley with the assurance that we will travel it without trouble because He is with us all the way. His rod and staff will comfort us, and we "will dwell in the house of the Lord for ever" (Ps. 23).

There is also the valley of despair and disappointment. What a barrier this deep abyss can be as we travel the road of life. You are a young athlete hoping to make a certain goal in your sport, and you don't quite have the ability; you prepare for a career, and there are no job openings; you enter a business that looks promising, and market conditions cause it to fail; you fall in love with someone who does not return your love; you marry and think all is going well, and suddenly you are asked for a divorce. There are so many deep ravines, rocky canyons, and deep eroded places that can block our progress. And often we come to them very unexpectedly and feel there is no way we can ever get across to continue our journey.

Isaiah certainly had known many of these seemingly impossible barriers in his life. His people had been defeated and carried into captivity and slavery. Yet he had discovered by faith that valleys shall be lifted up so that we can make safe crossing, and mountains brought low so we can get over them. We read often of people who have overcome paralysis, survived prison camps, and found their way through depression with the guidance of the same God that Isaiah knew could make the "uneven ground . . . become level" (RSV). There is no problem too great, no disappointment too deep but that our God can "cut and fill" and make for us, through the desert, a highway.

I think for many of us the valley of fear is the most difficult one of all. In my desire to be a minister, my fear of speaking in public was one of my greatest barriers. It is a rather natural fear and has not entirely left me, but through the years I have learned that my fear comes from being self-conscious when I should be more God conscious. As He has helped turn my thoughts toward Him and other people and away from myself, the fear has faded—that deep valley has been filled and lifted up.

In a period of illness and depression, a few years ago, I thought I was going to die. Then slowly I began to realize that death was not my enemy. It was the *fear* of death that tormented me. Over and over I began to recite in my mind my favorite Scriptures that give assurance of God's guidance through the death experience; over and over I reviewed the words of favorite hymns that promise that God will be my Companion on the passage. And as the fear was taken away, that valley seemed to be lifted up, and the hills over which I could not see seemed to be brought low. I love and enjoy this life on earth, and I am grateful that I have been granted some more years of good health. But I know they are limited years, and I believe that when I do come to the last valley, a highway will be there.

The opposite of fear is not courage; the opposite of fear is faith. Courage is the assurance that we do not stand alone in the difficult moments of life. Fear comes when we live our life in front of a mirror, aware of ourselves and our problems. Courage comes when we live by a window through which we see the vast landscape of God's actions and become aware of His presence. "I will fear no evil: for thou art with me" (Ps. 23:4). Fear comes from forgetting

EVERY VALLEY LIFTED UP

who we are; courage is with the little boy sitting on the corral fence and knowing he is the beloved son of one who owns all that one can see.

Faith reminds us that some of the hills standing in our way are not as high; some of the roads are not as steep as they appear from a distance or from the wrong perspective. One of the ways God has of bringing the mountains low is giving us the ability to see that most of the things we fear never happen, and they disappear or become less difficult as we approach them with faith and reason. Often as I approach a difficult challenge I like to remember that day on the Snake River plain when the impossibly steep grade up to the Danskin Mountains became less and less fearsome as I got closer to it, and it became quite possible when I actually started to climb it.

Often as I approach steep mountain roads, I like to "lift up my eyes to the hills" and remind myself that "My help comes from the Lord," who made the hills (Ps. 121). He knows the way to get through them and over them. As I enjoy pleasant travel on fine highways through the mountains, I like to watch for the cuts, the fills, the bridges that make it all possible, and ponder the faith of Isaiah who pictured it so well: "Every valley shall be lifted up, and every mountain and hill be made low" (RSV).

11

Any Bush Will Do!

"The bush was burning, yet it was not consumed" (Ex. 3:2, RSV).

This past October I had the privilege of spending a few days in the mountains of central Idaho. It was a time of remembering; it was a time for long thoughts about the meaning of life. The autumn hills were beautiful. The weather was ideal. The fall colors were at their best. This is the country to which Betty and I came over forty years ago to begin our ministry after graduation from seminary. It was here in the small town of Salmon and the vast and beautiful country around it that we spent twenty years, pastored a loving congregation, raised our family, and formed many of the values by which we live. I spent a few days camped out, with just my horse, near the mountain ranch where once I lived for several years. The ranch is now the home and way of life for our daughter and her family.

I spent my days riding the familiar trails, visiting favorite springs and streams, and seeing again the well-remembered scenes. I felt very much at home. These sparsely populated areas do not change as do our more urban areas. Due to good range management the grass was more abundant; young trees I remembered had grown tall; in addition to deer, an elk herd has developed in the area. But in general, change was slight. There is an eternal quality about the hills. They change with the seasons but not much with the years.

On a bright morning, looking at sunlight bursting through a clump of aspen trees, I was reminded of an instance many years ago when first I met these mountains. I was riding up a ridge toward the rising sun when the sunlight, shining directly through a small tree, caught my attention. Heavy dew had left droplets of clear water on the brilliant fall colors of the tree. The refracted light through the droplets, the rays of the rising sun around and above the tree with the sun itself hidden, and the flaming fall colors of the leaves all combined in a glorious blaze. Truly I saw a bush that burned and was not consumed by the flame.

My mind jumped back across the hundreds of years to someone who was doing much as I was doing. Moses was out in the hills and he was pondering his career—his life work—seeking God's guidance. In this setting and in this moment of wonder, Moses saw more than a burning bush. He sensed the power and wonder of God and the fact that God has purposes for our lives. He said: "I will turn aside and see this great sight" (Ex. 3:3, RSV). Then he realized that God had a message for him and that he was standing on holy ground.

Recalling so vividly my experience of more than forty years ago gave me a feeling of assurance, remembering how that moment and similar experiences have helped me through the years to have a sense of purpose in life and a confidence of God's presence that could sustain me even in the times when it seemed that God was far away. I believe that each person who is looking for it will find his or her own burning bush. For that bush can be any bush—it is the place and time when we become aware that God is speaking to us in an intimate and personal way and that our lives are in His hands.

A man who was very interested in the church made a trip to Europe. He was eager to see the place where Martin Luther had lived and worked; he wanted to see where John Wesley, the founder of the Methodist church, had lived, preached, and been converted. He desired to see Aldersgate Street, where Wesley had worshiped, and many other places important in church history. But when this man came home from his trip he was disappointed and made a very interesting comment. He said, "I went to see these great shrines of our faith, and they were just ordinary places, just ordinary places." This is a great insight into truth because we need always to remember that God comes to ordinary people like us, and He comes in ordinary places. It is not the kind of bush or the way it burns that makes the soil around it holy ground. It is the knowledge of the presence of God and having ears to hear and eyes to see. Then any bush will do when in it we see the work of God and through the experience become aware of His guidance.

I often see advertisements for trips to the Holy Land suggesting that we go to see the places of the Bible, places where prophets spoke and above all the place where Christ was born and lived and taught. I am sure this would be a rewarding experience. I would like to retrace the travels of the apostle Paul. But the truly great experience for the Christian is not to see where Christ

ANY BUSH WILL DO!

came into the world two thousand years ago. It is to find the place where Christ comes into your life now, today, in your present situation, in your home, your church, beside your very ordinary bush where there can surely be some holy ground.

It was after I was grown, and my mother was old, that she told me of a special place in her life. During the very worst days of the Great Depression when she had almost no money, children to care for, constant work without modern conveniences and appliances, and the ever-pressing fear of "losing the farm"—it was in these dark days that Mother found a source of strength in her faith. She had a place by a haystack, sheltered from the wind, where she could go by herself when she could find some free moments. And there, she said, she went to weep and pray. I think it was her burning bush. Beside that haystack she found herself on holy ground and met the One who could help her through another day.

There is the classic story of the orphan girl who prays each night for a rich couple to come and take her to their expensive home and adopt her as their own. But they never come. Once she is taken for a trial period and then returned to the orphanage. She overhears what she is not supposed to hear: "She isn't very pretty, and we don't think she is very bright." And then one day a very ordinary couple come. They take her to a very plain and ordinary house and love her in an ordinary way, and she grows up as a common, ordinary beloved daughter. And I am sure that in later years she would go back to that very common old house and stand a while on holy ground—the place where she had seen her burning bush. Many of our favorite hymns are those written by someone who saw a burning bush, who remembered a time and place when they realized the love of God, a love that is given even if we are not very pretty, perhaps not very bright, and not even very good.

There was a man who had two sons. We read the story in the fifteenth chapter of Luke. The younger son blew his money, messed up his life, lost his job, finally found himself feeding pigs, and even considering eating the food the pigs ate. Then something wonderful happened. His burning bush, I think, was beside a pigpen. That's where the son started his journey back to his father's house. And I suspect if we had the rest of the story we would find him sometime returning to that unlikely place to stand a while on holy ground.

For some the burning bush may be a thing of beauty or power, bright morning sun shining through bright dew-pearled autumn leaves. For some it may be a difficult experience that turns a life around. It may be a very scrubby bush, an oversized weed that we can't pull out of our gardens. Maybe it is loneliness, fear, a broken home, a business failure, or a time of illness. But when it turns our thoughts toward God and we hear Him speaking to us and giving us a new direction and a sense of purpose, we know we have seen our burning bush. And when we see God in it, any bush will do.

12

Streetlights and Headlights

"Thy word is a lamp unto my feet, and a light unto my path"
(Ps. 119:105).

The writer of Psalm 119 made a great discovery—the importance of a light, however small, that one can carry with him. If you have ever been out in the hills on a really dark night and on a rough trail, you know this from your own experience. The psalmist speaks of God's guidance as "a lamp unto my feet, and a light unto my path." It doesn't need to light up the whole country, but it is adequate for the next step, and it is there when we need it. And it is a lamp we carry with us, not one that is fixed to a certain place or time. Some people think they can predict the future by the past, but there is a good reason to doubt this. On a dark night we are not helped a lot by a light that shines on the place where we were the night before.

As I have traveled on some very dark nights on mountain trails, I have realized that the smallest of lights that I can carry with me is worth more than the greatest light in the world that shines only in one place. In life we always travel a path we have not walked before. We really cannot see very far ahead, and sometimes we must travel in a lot of darkness. But a light that is adequate for the next step is adequate for the entire journey if we carry it with us because as we move ahead, the light moves and lights as much of the path as we really have to have lighted.

There are two kinds of people, headlight people and streetlight people. Because a streetlight is brighter, sometimes wonderfully bright, there are people who want to stay always within its glow. But it is terribly limited. A headlight or flashlight may not be so bright, but because it goes with us there is no limit to where we can travel with it. There are individuals, families, and even churches that are streetlight people. They do not want to leave a known tradition; they have found something good and fear to venture by faith in search of something better. Headlight people have found that they can venture into the dark, carrying a light with them, and there will always be enough light as they go along. There is then no limit to their freedom and possibility of adventure.

When I was a teenager we moved from the farm into town for one year, and in the evenings a group of us would play under a streetlight. Our playing field was always limited by the area covered by the streetlight. Later as I learned to drive a car, I discovered that even though the headlights were not too bright, I could travel for miles on the darkest country roads because I carried the light with me. I have been out in the forest on a very dark night without a flashlight. I have found a campfire very comforting, but I have wished I could carry it with me to find my way back to my hunting camp, my tent, my friends, and a warm supper, something I could do with a very little flashlight.

STREETLIGHTS AND HEADLIGHTS

Too often we want to see the trail for many yards ahead before we take the next step, and what a limitation that puts on us. Perhaps this is why we are afraid of the dark. How liberating it is when we find that the little lamp of faith, though it only lights the trail for one or two steps, will go with us and will light the next step and the next, and, in fact, light the whole distance and bring us safely home. If we lack the faith to take the step ahead that is lighted for us, then the lamp stops moving, and the way ahead stays dark. Sometimes I wonder why God doesn't give me more light on the way ahead, and the reason is that I am standing still, afraid to walk in the light He has already given me.

In our modern world we take for granted the headlights on our cars and forget what wonderful things they are. They are designed so that we can see what we need to see at any given moment if we travel at a reasonable speed. But they are really very limited when we are stopped. If we are stopped for too long the headlights grow weaker, and the battery runs down. Headlights are for people who are going somewhere.

Many years ago I conducted an evening worship service in a schoolhouse near the upper end of the Pahsimeroi Valley in East Central Idaho. This was before any electrical lines reached into this remote area, and the few scattered ranch homes still used oil and gas lamps. After the service I came out into an extremely dark night, and the thirty miles down the valley were composed of one vast sea of darkness. Except for a dark road leading into the darkness, there was no indication of direction, no suggestion of a way through all the empty blackness. But as I drove down the valley, every inch of the way was lighted as I needed it. My headlights were sufficient because they were lights I carried with me. If I had been afraid to start because I could not see ahead for more than a short distance, then the road would never have been lighted.

The drive down that beautiful valley is more pleasant in daylight or bright moonlight, but life does not always allow us the pleasant way, and much of our journey has to be in the dark. God does not reveal to us all that is ahead, but He does ask us to go boldly with faith in the light we have, making sure we carry it with us.

I worked briefly in a mine where I used a light that was fastened to my hard hat—truly a headlight. This light not only traveled with me giving me light when I needed it, but, being attached to my head, it automatically turned with my head and lighted whatever I turned to look at without my even thinking about it. My light always lighted the area I needed to work on and showed me what I needed to see. But it was not a satisfactory light for someone else to work by, and I could never do good work depending on another person's light.

I have noticed this same effect to some extent when I have walked a dark path at night with two or more people and with only one flashlight. When we are trying to walk or work by someone else's light, there is always a shadow in the way, or the light is not shining where it is needed just at that moment one needs it. Surely the faith of other people can be a help at times, but it is never a substitute for a faith of our very own, which, like the miner's hat lamp, becomes a part of us and moves with every move we make.

I like the personal pronoun in the psalm: "Thy word is a lamp unto my feet, and a light unto my path." It is a light I carry with me. Because I carry it with me, I can travel on the darkest night. It shines where I need it, it moves ahead when I move ahead, it stops with me when I need to stop and examine something. I do not have to run to keep up with it, and with it I can dare to take the first step on a long dark journey.

13

The Turkey Trap

Long ago I heard or read a turkey story. If it has been published I would like to give credit for it, but I have forgotten where it came from. It may be the sort of story that is simply part of our folklore. I am sure it is not original with me. I don't know if it is true, but if it isn't it ought to be. It concerns a man who lived in the hills where there were wild turkeys. Each year as part of his Thanksgiving Day celebration, the man went into the hills and caught his Thanksgiving turkey. He had a very unique turkey trap. It was simply a very large, heavy wooden box. One end of the box was propped up with a stick. A string attached to the stick was stretched out to some nearby bushes where the man could hide and wait for a turkey. Long lines of corn were laid out reaching from the woods to the box, and more corn was placed under the box for additional bait. When a turkey followed a line of corn to the box and then stopped to eat corn under the box, the man simply jerked out the stick; the box fell and trapped the turkey.

A few days before Thanksgiving he prepared his trap

THE TURKEY TRAP

and waited. Soon a fine gobbler followed a string of corn into the trap. The man was just ready to pull the string when another turkey entered the trap and then another. More turkeys were coming, and he could not decide when to pull the string. Just when there were ten turkeys in the trap, they suddenly flew. The man quickly pulled the string, but all he got was the first big gobbler. It was a fine bird, very adequate for his dinner, as fine a bird as he had ever had. But his Thanksgiving was ruined. He was unable to give thanks for the turkey he had because he was thinking so much about his misfortune: the loss of nine turkeys. He complained. He moped. It was all he could think about, the way in which his plans had failed and circumstances had robbed him of nine turkeys.

Quite often we hear people complain about what they could have had *if:* if they had just sold out sooner, if they had invested when they were younger, if they had gone into another line of work. They bemoan the loss of that which they never really had anyway, any more than the man had the nine turkeys that flew away. This pessimistic way of looking at things is a tendency we can avoid if we simply remember to be thankful for what we do have and enjoy the turkey that didn't get away.

A most important gift of the Christian faith is the gift of gratitude. Giving thanks and rejoicing in the gift of life is fundamental to true worship. Rejoicing and giving thanks, like laughter, helps keep us healthy. Paul wrote: "Rejoice in the Lord always; again I will say, Rejoice. . . . with thanksgiving let your requests be made known to God" (Phil. 4:4-6, RSV).

The idea that Christianity is more concerned with requiring obligation and duty than it is with rejoicing and thanksgiving is a sad misunderstanding. It should not be a primary concept of our faith. Obligation as a primary motive doesn't motivate very well. We will all do vastly more out of gratitude than we will out of obligation. What man will not do more for his wife because he loves her than because she is demanding, and enjoy doing it. A religion of commitment and obligation, without gratitude and rejoicing, is a slave driver with a whip from which one will escape if he can. Churches that have trouble raising the budget are generally churches that are constantly putting obligations on the members without giving them much to be thankful for. When we are really grateful for something that has been done for us, we have a strong natural desire to give something, even if it can only be a big hug.

Some years ago a hunter was lost in the wilderness. The weather was cold; it was snowing each night. After five days the official search was abandoned. But one man, with a good knowledge of the area, persisted and continued to search. He found the lost hunter, still in fairly good condition. The overjoyed hunter insisted on giving the searcher, who had not been seeking any reward other than saving the man, a very expensive rifle. He was reacting in a most normal way: he had to give to express his gratitude.

Why is there so much grumbling instead of rejoicing, so much complaining instead of thanksgiving? Is it because we have so much that we complain over what has been lost or not yet attained? Often those who have much complain most, and those who are most thankful are those who have never had more than one turkey in the trap. When I was close to the cattle business, I noticed it

THE TURKEY TRAP

was the rancher with a large herd who complained loudest over a drop in cattle prices. The person who loses his perspective on life and becomes hard to live with because of a drop in the stock market is generally one who has more than enough to live on and something left over to invest. When we have almost everything we need and most of what we have ever wanted, it is hard to remember that we came into the world with nothing but the gift of life itself, and we will leave with only the precious promise of eternal life and a God who loves us—the things for which we truly rejoice and give thanks.

In our family my older sisters were eager for a little brother, and when he was being expected they asked my mother: "If it is a boy will he be wearing overalls?" He came, and he wasn't—not even overalls. And that's how we all arrive. The world does not owe us a living, so every day we can rejoice and give thanks for anything and everything we have. The practice of thanksgiving can protect us from becoming bitter and despondent over what we have lost or never attained. It's easy to get our values mixed up.

A rather exciting event in my teen years is still impressed on my memory. With another boy I was fishing from a small rowboat in the Snake River. An older man, wearing waders, had gone out from the shore, slipped off into deep water, and was helpless and in danger of drowning. With our boat we quite easily helped him out, simply by having him grasp the back of the boat while we rowed into shallow water. His first comment when he got safely to shore was revealing: "Thank God, my tobacco's dry!" At least he gave thanks. Perhaps life without tobacco was unthinkable.

Sometimes it takes a shock or a traumatic experience to make us appreciate what we have. This is the theme of Dorothy Johnson's story "The Hanging Tree." A man goes West to search for gold. He has a passion for gold; everything else in his life is pushed aside. He doesn't have time for family or friends. Gold is all that is important. Then he finds gold, a rich strike with lots of easy gold. He is accumulating his gold when he is accused of a crime and sentenced to hang. The rope is over the branch of the tree, and the noose is ready for his neck. At the very last moment he is saved from hanging, but others get his gold. The man loses his gold but finds his life and finds there is much more to live for than gold. These are lines of the theme song from the movie: "I walked away from the hanging tree, and my own true love she walked with me." And there was far more real joy in finding his life and his love than he ever had in finding his gold.

It is sad if we must lose, or nearly lose, the most precious things we have before we realize how precious they really are. Every new morning is a fresh new gift. In a very real sense, every new day we walk away from the hanging tree and walk away with adventure, love, and goodness all around us.

It is a good thing to constantly train our lips to say thank you. Giving is so much fun that it would be nice to have a great deal to give away. But the way life is we don't generally have a chance to give away as much as we receive, so it is important to learn how to receive with gratitude. If we cannot receive with thanksgiving it is a sign we have never learned how to give with joy.

Lack of gratitude is the mark of colossal conceit because it indicates that we think no one else has contrib-

THE TURKEY TRAP

uted to what we have or what we have accomplished. We think our good fortune has occurred because of our own cleverness, strength, brilliance, or hard work. We fail to see how indebted we are to God and other people. If we do give thanks it is to thank God that we are not like other people.

Lack of gratitude brought one of the sharpest rebukes from the mouth of Jesus. He met ten lepers. Nine were from His own religious community. He healed all ten. They went on their way, and only one came back and thanked Him for the healing. You can almost hear the disappointment in Jesus' voice when He asked: "Where are the nine? Was no one found to return and give praise to God except this foreigner?" (Luke 17:117-18, RSV). What a sad commentary on His own people. Perhaps because they believed themselves God's chosen people, they thought they deserved the healing. Instead of giving thanks they were concerned with complaining over the years they had lost in the leper colony.

We come into life helpless; we go from life helpless. For a few years in between we may be able to carry our own weight, maybe even help other people a little bit, but never will we balance the scales. Always we will be deeply in debt, and the only way we can settle the account is through our gratitude. Too many people think that admitting their dependence is a sign of weakness, perhaps humiliating. Actually the opposite is true. There is a great difference between being humble and being humiliated.

The little boy who looks up at his father and says "My daddy can do anything" has complete faith in what his father can do. He is rejoicing in his father's love. This little boy is humble, but he is not humiliated. He is very proud. He says, "This is my daddy." And when we can look up to God and know that He can do all things, and we give thanks to Him, we are humble but we are not humiliated. We are very proud that we can say, "Our Father." If we prosper we can give to others with thanksgiving; if we have misfortune we can accept our difficulties with thanksgiving because we know that giving and receiving are two sides of the same coin. As we understand that all things are in God's hands, we can get life in the right perspective.

I am glad that we have a custom of a national day for thanksgiving. It can be a day of real rejoicing and giving serious thought to the fine art of receiving and the importance of gratitude in all areas of life. Homes can be brightened, and husband-wife, parent-child, and brother-sister relationships improved, if we practice the art of saying, "Thank you, I really do appreciate what you have done for me."

There are two kinds of people: those who think they are giving more than they get and those who know they are getting more than they give. The first kind can never be truly happy. Always they are concerned and worried for fear that someone is taking advantage of them, that they are being shortchanged. The second kind can never really be unhappy because they know that whatever happens, they are really getting more than they have earned.

These two kinds of people are easily separated in a time of misfortune. At the time of the Great Depression in the thirties, those who thought they were giving more than they were getting could not face up to the crash. Some committed suicide, some had nervous breakdowns,

THE TURKEY TRAP

some simply became so morose and unsociable no one could live with them. They never could quite cope. But those people who knew that they were receiving more than they were giving were able to put their arms around family members and say, "Thank God we still have each other." They were able to say, "Thank God there is tomorrow and a chance for another start." They were able to say, "Thank God for our faith." They were the ones who came through and who rebuilt their lives.

The secret of the good life is just as simple as the lesson of the turkey trap. It is learning to rejoice over what we have rather than complaining about the turkeys that flew away.

14

Chasing Donkeys

When Saul was "discovered" by Samuel, recognized as the person God wanted to serve as the king of Israel, anointed, and elevated to that high position that would have been the dream of any young man in the kingdom, he was not seeking the position. As a dutiful son of his father, Kish, Saul was out in the hills trying to round up his father's stray donkeys (1 Sam. 9—10). Saul was tall and handsome, likely a fine athlete. He was probably aware of his ability, but it had never gone to his head. He was not out trying to be a king. He was loyal to his father and doing his very best in the work that had been assigned to him. He was considerate of others. After several days when Saul and the servant with him had not found the donkeys, he realized that his father would be more concerned about his well-being than about the donkeys. It was while he was sincerely trying to work out this everyday problem, in this rather ordinary assignment, that Saul was introduced to Samuel and discovered his real destiny: God had called him to be a king.

With his good looks, talent, ability, and popularity

CHASING DONKEYS

Saul might well have considered the job of rounding up his father's donkeys a pretty poor assignment. He might have thought he was cut out for pro football or Hollywood or politics and been seeking some special fortune instead of accepting the work assigned to him. But the fascination of the story, and the great truth it tells us about life, lies in the fact that Saul did what he was asked to do and very earnestly tried to locate the stray donkeys, never once indicating that he considered it a job unworthy of a young man of his talents. And it is this seemingly unimportant job, this acceptance of the obligations and responsibilities present in the place and circumstance in which he found himself, that led Saul to something more than he would ever have hoped for or dreamed about.

This is certainly a parable for all of us who feel sometimes that we are burdened with uneventful and unrewarding tasks: caring for a family, holding down a job, or running a business. It is in the everyday doing of our duty that we find our destiny; it is only as we do well what we have been given to do that we move through the paths and hills of life to really find what God has in store for us. We are much more likely to find happiness when we are seeking some other objective as part of a busy life than if we are looking for happiness. Saul found a kingdom while looking for donkeys; had he been looking for a kingdom with no other goal in life, the chances are he would have found only donkeys.

Our folktales and fables are filled with this theme simply because it is so true to real life. It is Cinderella and not the scheming stepsister who becomes the queen. The stepsisters tried hard enough at queen seeking, but nothing else. It is the young man or woman who goes to college sincerely seeking a good education who is most likely to find there the right person to marry and fulfill the dream of a good home.

When we study the lives of people who have had great experiences, who have made contributions to civilization, who have found satisfying careers, it is amazing how often these people never really dreamed that the job they were doing was the one that would lead to the reward and satisfaction that they have found in life. They were people who went ahead with faith and did the task at hand with a sense of adventure. Being in the right place at the right time is a lot more than fate. It is generally the result of being employed with a good will in the job you have been given, even if it seems that you are just chasing donkeys. A stray donkey can lead one into some beautiful country.

The stories of my childhood generally began with a young person setting out to seek his or her fortune. This is true even of the story of the three little pigs—they went out to seek their fortunes. They didn't know what they would find. There was no job-placement agency and certainly no guaranteed minimum salaries. But they did set out. They didn't just sit and wait.

This is very basic to our Christian life, this sense of adventure in which we go out, not necessarily knowing what we will find, but with faith and expectation. Perhaps the best way to get the job you want is to take the job you can get; it can at least help keep you in shape for the better job when it comes along, and you're bound to learn something. Of all the kings of his time, Saul may have been the one who knew most about tracking donkeys. It may have come in handy in his military exploits, and it certainly would have been a help in illustrating his polit-

CHASING DONKEYS

ical speeches. Saul never guessed that tracking donkeys would lead to a king's crown, but it did.

Too often in our time we want to be so sure of what we are getting before we start out that we are too long about starting. This is a lack of faith not only in ourselves but in God. If our first interest in a new job is the retirement benefit, the chances are we will never enjoy that benefit. A career counselor told me of a young man he worked with. The counselor asked: "What do you really want to be?" The young man said: "A retired rancher." There are some things to be said for that if one has sold the ranch for a good price, but the young man needed to recognize a lot of adventure in between where he was and where he wanted to be, and there needed to be a lot more emphasis on the "setting out" than on the arrival.

The retired ranchers I know who have had the most satisfaction in life generally started out digging postholes. Most of them didn't even get too much of the romantic part of being cowboys. In my part of the world, and in my experience, many of the most successful simply started out to improve their lives by joining the Civilian Conservation Corps of the Great Depression of the 1930s and giving it their best effort.

We never know what lies around the next corner, and we never find out until we "set out" with the faith that there is something good for us around that corner. A sadness of our time is the number of people who are listening to the preachers of the bad news, the news that says humanity is in control of the world and about to destroy it. Nothing in history bears this out, and certainly nothing in our Christian heritage. We have the good news. This has always been—and still is—God's world, and His goal is creation, not destruction, for His world and each of His people.

To find our destiny we should be prepared to meet what lies around the next corner and to meet it as opportunity and not as trouble. Too often we anticipate trouble instead of opportunity. An event in life is often one or the other simply by the way we look at it. I remember an elk-hunting trip where I found the trail blocked by down timber when I was packing into camp. My first reaction was disappointment. It meant a rather long and difficult detour. But it was on the detour that I got the elk I was looking for. The most challenging and productive appointment that I had during my career as a pastor followed the bitter disappointment of not getting the appointment I expected. But that disappointment left me free to go to a new church that was being started where I could share with the congregation in the building of a fine new church.

Around the next corner may be a burden we will have to carry that we would rather not carry. But it may also be the way in which we find talents we didn't know we had and find the real reason for why we were born.

Nathaniel Hawthorne was one of the great writers of American literature. There is the story of the dark day when he came home bitterly disappointed and had to tell his wife that he had lost his job. Her reply is one of the wonderful responses of a spouse in the history of the world. According to the story, she smiled and said: "Now you will have time to write the book that you have always wanted to write."

A favorite parable tells us that the kingdom of heaven is like a man who found a treasure hidden in a field

(Matt. 13:44). Having done some plowing, I have an idea that the man found the treasure because he was plowing the field, and the plow ran into buried treasure. At least I am going to assume that, and the story says that for joy he sold all he had and bought the field, so he obviously was a hired man out doing his job. He was plowing the field, which may have seemed to him a rather dull occupation. But he was doing it. He wasn't sitting under a tree dreaming about finding a hidden treasure. He wasn't even going over the field with his metal detector. He was plowing the field when he found his treasure, something he hadn't looked for and really didn't expect to find. And that is generally how life give us the good things.

One reason I like stream fishing better than lake fishing is because I can always believe that around the next bend in the stream there is the hole with the big trout in it. It isn't always so, or at least sometimes I don't have the right fly, but I can always anticipate that around the next bend there is something more exciting. It is this confidence that keeps me fishing, not wanting to leave until I make one more cast which, of course, can mean I stay pretty late. But it is a joy to be able to anticipate that which you do not see and anticipate it with the expectation that it will be good.

Most important to the good life is the assurance that whatever lies ahead around the corner, God will be there and will be involved in it. In Psalm 59:10 there is a line that has been translated several ways. All the translations affirm that "God in his steadfast love will meet me" (RSV). This means that He is way ahead of me on the trail of life. He will meet me at every corner. He precedes me, and I will never outrun Him. The future is unknown to me but not to God, who is in charge of things. On an unknown trail it is good to know there is someone ahead of you that you can depend on.

I remember the first time I found myself alone with a pack string of several animals in some very rough country in the central Idaho wilderness. I have never been a very good packer, and always before I had been in the company of someone who was. I was apprehensive. The trails were steep. Just what would I do if a pack slipped and a horse was in trouble? I thought I had everything well secured, but it was comforting to know that ahead of me on the trail, and within shouting distance, was a more experienced packer pulling another pack string. I knew he was an expert packer; he had been over the trail many times, and he understood horses and mules.

And in a bad place one of my packs did slip, and a horse was in trouble and in danger of being pulled off the trail, possibly to serious injury. The trail was narrow; I had no place to tie up the horse I was riding, and to leave her and go back to help the horse in trouble would mean she would move on down the trail and start the string moving, which would shove the tangled horse over the edge. So I called out, and the man ahead heard me and tied up; he came back and helped me.

What a comforting word, this promise from the Psalms. Our God precedes us and can meet us at every turn. We are not alone as we journey down this unknown trail of life that is filled with excitement, interesting things, and sometimes difficult challenges. We will never get ahead of God. In all times and in all places He will be there ahead of us, there to meet us if we need Him.

CHASING DONKEYS

As Christians we can be prepared to meet whatever comes as an opportunity and not a source of trouble. We will look ahead with expectation and hope even if the job that we are in seems like a donkey chase, knowing that even in this, as in the story of Saul, God may be leading us toward the very meaning and purpose of our lives.

15

Cooking with Leftovers

Few of us have a chance to live life on the basis of our first choices. This applies to where we live, our professions, our physical strength and stature, our health, our IQ's, and a great many other factors. Handicaps are not something other people have. There is a matter of degree, but in terms of what we really want—the ideal life—we are all handicapped, some a bit more than others. The secret of the good life is not in having everything we want but in doing everything we can with what we have. And the wonder of the Christian faith is in its power to help us do that.

A fine thing about the game of golf is the fact that one does not have to play up to any particular standard of excellence in order to enjoy it. Players establish their handicap and then find joy and challenge in seeing how well they can play in relation to that handicap. One can play a great game, even if he is not a great player in comparison with a pro, because he plays his very best with the handicap he has.

I think that God's score card in life is kept in the same

COOKING WITH LEFTOVERS

manner. Life does not give us the perfect shots—it requires that we make the best of difficult shots and our own limitations. When I was young and agile I wanted to get involved in rodeo. But I couldn't afford a horse, much less an entry fee. Now I have a horse, but my back hurts. When I was in high school and the football season came around, I would have given anything to weigh 175 pounds instead of 128. Now I weigh 175 pounds and want to weigh a good deal less.

The New Testament account of the life and work of the apostle Paul gives us many brief but revealing glimpses that tell a story. One brief comment, Acts 16:7, was the basis of a fine biblical novel written many years ago: *The Road to Bithynia.* "When they had come opposite Mysia, they attempted to go into Bithynia, but the Spirit of Jesus did not allow them; so, passing by Mysia, they went down to Troas" (RSV). It was while on this unplanned detour that Paul received his call to go to Macedonia, and from this came some of the finest work of his career. But that wasn't what he had asked for. Obviously, Paul's first choice was Bithynia, and tradition tells us that Bithynia was a very desirable place to live and work.

The greatness of Paul lies in his ability to do a great work in the place that was a second choice. He didn't let disappointment keep him from doing his best to serve. Knowing Paul's character and determination, we can be sure he did his best to get to Bithynia. We also know that Paul lived a great life and did his great work in spite of a severe handicap that he called his "thorn in the flesh," a thorn that was never removed for him.

The test of a really good cook is not what can be done under ideal conditions with a tender standing rib roast or fine T-bone steaks. It takes some doing to really foul these up. But the test of a great cook is what can be done with the odds and ends left over from yesterday's meal. To make this an attractive, nourishing meal, working only with what one has available, is a challenge. There was a family on a camping trip. They became isolated in the mountains by a flash flood. The children had never considered their mother a great cook even though she had consistently put good food on the table at home. But after several days without supplies, when they were really feeling hunger pains, and the children discovered what she could do with porcupine meat and dandelion greens, they recognized her cooking talent and for years boasted of her ability.

When I was growing up there was a certain item my mother cooked that I considered a great treat. We called it a dough gob. My mother took scraps of dough from her bread baking, fried them in a certain way, and flavored them. They are among the pleasant memories of my childhood. My mother was raised as an aristocrat in Scotland. I'm sure she never even dreamed that she would be raising her children in quite rough conditions on a farm in the American West during the Great Depression. If she could have had her way, dough gobs would not have been her idea of a special treat for her children. But I constantly give thanks for the fact that she knew how, and found the source of strength and courage to work and serve in "Troas" when she found the road to her "Bithynia" closed.

Any of us who really live know what it means to dream of being the star player and then sit out most of the season trying to be a good substitute. This is what life is all

COOKING WITH LEFTOVERS

about, learning to make great harmony playing second fiddle, doing our best work in an assignment we didn't ask for.

Faith enables us to cope with disappointment and make a good and nutritious meal out of yesterday's leftovers—a faith that makes us confident that God has a purpose for us in the situation we didn't expect or ask for.

In my own career some of the best experiences have come when I did not get to do what I wanted to do. I have always liked the out-of-doors, undeveloped country, and pioneering people. After I graduated from seminary, it was my dream to go to Alaska. My bishop, who was a good friend and counselor as well as bishop, served Alaska and Idaho. He simply said he did not want to send Betty and me with a tiny baby into any of the situations that he had available in Alaska at that time. Instead he sent us to a very challenging situation in the mountains of central Idaho. There we spent twenty years in what was very rewarding work, and I have been forever thankful it worked out that way. Looking back I feel sure that my first choice would not have been so good.

Then, after the years in that rural setting in Salmon, Idaho, where we developed the Salmon River Larger Parish, there came a time when I should move from that church. But I was restless and found it hard to settle for a more typical and established church appointment. With two brothers who were lawyers and a lifelong interest in legal matters, I had a dream of doing something in law and politics. With three children at various stages in education and a wife who would like to complete her college work, I hit on a great idea. We had accumulated a little property. We could sell what we had and would have enough, if we were frugal, to move to the university town where I had graduated, rent a house, and all five of us could be students while I went through law school. The university had a very highly acclaimed school of law. So with great expectation I visited the university to apply to the law school, thinking that there were no problems since I had graduated there twenty-five years earlier with a good record.

To my great disappointment I was not accepted. It was pointed out to me that there were many more applicants than the law school could accommodate, and they could not give a place to a student who had less than half of a normal law career ahead of him.

My dream came tumbling down along with the realization I wasn't young anymore. I really hadn't thought of that before. But it did leave me free to accept the challenge of building a new church on the growing edge of Boise. And the fourteen years we spent before retirement helping to develop the Hillview United Methodist Church were years I would not want to trade for any other experience.

Over a thousand people united with the church during that time, we made a host of good friends, and we can look at that fine church today with a great sense of satisfaction. It is hard for me to believe that anything I might have achieved as a lawyer could have been so rewarding, but I had to have a door slammed in my face in order to find my way. Through it all it was an abiding faith that whatever worked out would work out for the best that kept Betty and me looking forward during a time of change. And it was faith that helped us see that the Hillview Church, which had been started, was in

COOKING WITH LEFTOVERS

debt, failing, and about to be abandoned as a mission project, was a challenge and an opportunity that would fit our style of ministry better than a comfortable, well-established church.

Faith is always the most important ingredient in making a good nutritious meal out of yesterday's leftovers. When we are confident that God is with us and our work is worthwhile, our perspective of the situation will change from a second choice to a great adventure. The disappointment that Paul experienced when he was denied his dream of Bithynia was soon forgotten when he found how much there was to do in Macedonia. And faith in his mission to Macedonia would eliminate any regrets and grieving Paul might have done over the loss of Bithynia.

God has given us another wonderful talent for working with leftovers—the gift of imagination. This is the kind of sight that enables us to look—after the fire—at the ashes of our dream house and see a new and better house standing in its place. Imagination is closely related to inspiration. Positive thinking is simply the right use of imagination. Without imagination we can only work with what is; imagination shows us what might be, which is the first step to discovering what can be.

My love of mountains, forests, streams, and wild animals started at an early age. I grew up on a flat farm with no mountains, no forests, and no rushing streams. But I had imagination, a natural part of childhood, and it is a part of my childhood that I hope has never died. We lived in irrigated country, so a dredge had been used to dig a drainage ditch. On one side of the ditch were large piles of gravel which became my mountains. The drain ditch ran clear, and small fish we called chubs became my trout and steelhead. Cattails along the ditch were my forest trees, and I reveled in being a mountain man.

I never knew we were poor; I know I was not underprivileged. I have always been thankful that no one ever tried to discourage my imagination, and throughout my life it has helped me see opportunities where some others have seen only obstacles. In the churches I have served, imagination has enabled me to see the church as it could be, and it has given us a pattern for moving in that direction.

I love to watch children at play. An old packing box becomes a house, a row of rocks a boundary, or an old drape a king's robe or an evening gown. When Jesus said we must become as little children, in addition to trust maybe He had in mind imagination.

When Paul was denied his dream of Bithynia, he did not spend time feeling sorry for himself. I have always liked the brevity of that account. Paul dealt with his disappointment in one brief entry, and in the very next lines in the account he gave us a clue to the gift that can save us from self-pity. He at once became concerned about the needs of the people of Macedonia.

God gave to him and gives to us all the cure for self-pity: other people to care for. This is the best medicine for frustration or sorrow. It keeps us from turning our lives inward on ourselves. Here is a great example of a well-directed life: to have a great disappointment, to deal with it with one brief entry in the journal of life, and then move on to concern for others. In times of crisis and hardship, those who are deeply involved in helping each other are the ones who weather the storm themselves.

In the darkest days of the Great Depression, I know

COOKING WITH LEFTOVERS

there were times when my parents might well have given in to despair and spent their time counting their losses. But we did have a little house in which to eat and sleep. I remember a transient family that came to our rural area with no place at all for shelter. My parents and others at once set about cleaning and repairing an unused chicken coop which sheltered the family for many months. It wasn't much of a home, but it was better than nothing.

I know that those who worked to provide it and helped care for the children found some real solace for their own hurting, and they were able to sleep better at night. One of the children of the chicken coop died, and my mother provided the simple but meaningful burial service since, with no money, they would not ask a stranger. Those years of good crops and no markets brought bitter disappointment to farmers trying to pay for a farm. But my parents survived, while some who cared only about their own troubles did not. God gives us other people to care about as an all-important way of dealing with our own hurts.

It is only natural that we all have our dreams of paradise, our idea of life as we want to live it. Anyone who lives with adventure will find disappointment; in this life we live a long way east of Eden. Those who are confident that God is guiding them and who use His wonderful gift of imagination to see possibilities, whose concern for others saves them from self-pity, do make remarkably nutritious and attractive meals out of unappetizing leftovers.

16

Fences

It is common to find a tree planted close to a building or a fence. It looks good for a year or two, but as the tree grows, the building or the tree or the fence suffers damage. A choice must be made; a tree too close to a house will suffer unsightly pruning or complete removal. It may be a lovely tree that is cherished. I once had a beautiful spruce tree planted near a fence that divided our front yard from our backyard. As the tree grew it crowded the fence, and the fence began to mar the symmetry of the tree. Rather than mutilate the tree I moved the fence. I am glad it was not on a property line, though even there we might have worked out a compromise, so that owners on each side could continue to enjoy that gracious growing spruce.

There are values in life that are more important than some of the arbitrary fences we have built around areas of our lives. Yet sometimes we become so accustomed to our fences that we find them hard to move, even if they are limiting our growth. We value them only because they have always been there, even if their reason for being has become meaningless or even hurtful. There is something very interesting about fences. I have lived with them as long as I can remember, and they have either been fencing me in or fencing me out. Or I have been helping to fix them or build them or tear them down or move them. Fences affect our lives enough that one of our greatest poets, Robert Frost, wrote a poem about mending fences, "Mending Wall."

The way we look at fences says something about the way we look at life. Frost observed: "Something there is that doesn't love a wall." The ravages of time will work against a fence and sooner or later bring it down. At the end of a summer when I had tried to keep the fence repaired between my place and a neighbor who didn't have adequate feed for his cattle, I wrote a poem about fences. My comment, after a tiring day of working on my fence, was: "I know I'll never build a fence so stout/that it can keep his starving cattle out" (from *Ranchland Poems*).

I remember a real estate transaction where some lots were being sold off the edge of a large cattle ranch. With several thousand acres of land in a ranch, one's attitude toward a fence line is very different than if he has a fifty-two-foot lot. The surveyor found that one lot sold off the edge of one ranch actually extended onto land the neighboring rancher had assumed was his and was not for sale. It took quite a bit of arbitration to resolve the problem. In an area of large ranches and rough terrain this is not uncommon. If one is dealing with a city building lot, a few feet become very important.

It was quite customary in the mountains where we used to live to have the fences built where it was convenient rather than exactly on the property line. A rocky area, a deep gully, or a bog by a spring—these were all reasons to change the location of a fence. But after a fence has been in place for many years, people have a very natural tendency to confuse the fence line with the property line, and serious arguments have resulted.

In many areas of the West where private property is often adjacent to public lands, there is a constant ongoing program dealing with boundaries. Early-day ranchers and homesteaders put fences as near their property lines as was convenient or possible. When everyone understood and land was cheap, it worked fine, but when people started subdivisions and made new surveys, interesting things often resulted. In one instance a man had a fine new home built and then discovered that the boundary of a national forest went right through the living room. It is interesting how we will confuse an established fence with a property line and try to argue and defend it, not recognizing that fences are often where they are because of convenience, the location often quite arbitrary.

This also is true of many of our customs, our way of thinking about other people, our actions, our eating habits, and our religious practices. We build fences in regard to the way we do things and the way we think; we become comfortable with these boundaries, but sometimes they are not consistent with what is best for our lives. They can even keep us from loving someone who might really be quite lovable if we could move our fence a little, or at least see over it, or build a gate. In a maturing Christian life we keep discovering that God has some survey markers that don't always agree with the fences that Grandfather built, or even some that we built earlier in life.

FENCES

Marriages that last through the years are those where couples have learned there are values more important than certain personal fence lines, and they have worked together moving some fences, sometimes even relocating a corner post. Surely this is one of the most rewarding and necessary activities we have in a growing family as parents and children work together on making needed adjustments on the fence lines that do give needed definition to our lives.

This doesn't mean we simply "let down the bars." That is another interesting phrase. It is sad when a person tries to tear down all his or her fences just because some don't seem to be in the right place. Willingness to compromise, move a fence, or maybe put in a few more gates for easy access to a neighbor's house don't mean giving up our basic beliefs or the great principles of our faith. Truth is truth, love is love, kindness is kindness, and mercy is mercy. These are great benchmarks we should not remove, but from them we may find that we can make new and better surveys, and we may even have new and better instruments than our fathers and mothers had.

Old fences can be very arbitrary. This was a constant struggle that Jesus had with religious leaders of His day. Starting from the benchmarks of God's love and mercy, Jesus asked the scribes and the Pharisees to move some of the fences they had built around much of the life of their times. And some of them were furious when He healed a man in violation of their sabbath rules (Luke 6:1-11).

Some of us have a hard time seeing a familiar fence moved even when we know it is in the wrong place. I once had some pigs that were fenced in with an electric fence—

a single wire that gives a nondangerous but sharp electric shock when it is touched. Pig bristles are good conductors, and the fence made a lasting impression on the pigs. I couldn't get them to cross that fence line even after the fence was removed. Those pigs gave me reason for some self-examination. A prejudice is an old fence line about which I am being pigheaded—an area of life I will not move into even when all reason for avoiding it has been removed.

It is easy to see when the other person's fence is in the wrong place. It is very difficult for us to see anything wrong with the places where we have built our fences, our customs, our way of doing things, and our standards for judging other people. It is important for us to examine our boundaries from time to time to see which of our fences are simply for our convenience or a matter of taste and fancy and those which really do mark boundaries that are important in the eyes of God and in keeping with the spirit and mind of Christ.

The neighbor with whom Robert Frost worked at mending the wall kept saying: "Good fences make good neighbors." And so it is where there are cows. Perhaps our fathers kept cows, but we do not. Frost rightly reflected that before he built a fence he'd find out what he was fencing in or fencing out.

And after fences have been built and in place for a very long time, we need to keep them under review. Some need to be repaired and maintained, but others may need to be moved or eliminated. Some old fences do nothing but limit what we can see from where we live; some only keep us from getting to know our neighbor whose friendship could be a bright spot in our lives. And some, like the fence that crowded my beautiful spruce tree, can cause us to grow in unattractive ways that are ugly and detract from what we ought to be.

17

Little Dog—Big Sled

When I was in grade school I walked some distance each day to a rural school. For part of the winter there was snow on the ground. I had read the dog stories of Jack London, and in my mind I had mushed across Alaska and the Yukon Territory. As I plodded through the snow I liked to picture myself driving a fine dog team which raced easily along while I just sat back and enjoyed the ride. I had a sled, and I had a dog—a rather strong but small dog of stock-dog breeding. It became obvious to me that my dog, who didn't have to work very hard for a living, might just as well give me a ride to school each day.

I made a dog harness out of old leather scraps and hitched my dog to the sled. He quite obediently pulled my sled around the yard. I added small amounts of weight to the sled, and he set himself to the task and willingly pulled them. Then came the critical test. I flopped myself on the sled and ordered him to mush. He gave it a good try and couldn't pull it—it was just too heavy for him. I ordered, exhorted, and scolded him, but we didn't move.

LITTLE DOG—BIG SLED

So I got a little willow switch for additional inducement. I ordered mush and applied the switch. He simply turned around and bit me. And he wasn't a mean dog; he was my friend. This was a perfect illustration of frustration.

I've remembered this through the years and thought of it often as I have faced situations that were too hard to handle. What that little dog needed was not a switch. He needed puppy chow or whatever it would take to make him into a bigger dog. He needed the power to become what he needed to be to handle the load that was given to him. Instead of that I was giving him punishment for not being a bigger, stronger dog.

This is a problem we see in religion that is legalistic or overly idealistic. It sets before us challenges saying you ought to do this, you ought to be a better person, *you ought to*. It gives the goals, the directions, and the rules without giving us the strength to carry out what is set before us. For this reason many of us, like my little dog, become frustrated and often growl and bite, even turning on people and causes we do care about.

Most of us don't need a religion to tell us what is wrong with us, to remind us of our smallness and weakness. We are all much aware of these problems already. We know we are not all we would like to be; we know we are not doing all the things we would like to do. My faithful dog and good companion always tried to do what I asked him to do. I am confident that he would have enjoyed pulling me to school on my sled. He just wasn't able!

As we face the tasks that we are given in life, what we are seeking is not exhortation and certainly not punishment for our weakness. We are longing for, and thankfully many are finding, a relationship with God that is giving us the power to become what we need to be in order to pull the load.

The heart of the Christian message, the good news of the gospel, is the truth that through faith we can become more than we presently are. One of the greatest lines of Scripture is the passage that says: "To all who received him, who believed in his name, he gave power to become children of God" (John 1:12, RSV). Whatever the challenge or the need or the grief or the problem that we are trying to pull or handle, God does not give us ridicule or punishment. He gives us power to become bigger and stronger. This is what we are really needing and seeking.

Our problem generally isn't lack of knowledge except as we deal with a technical question. It isn't lack of knowing right from wrong. It is the lack of power to become what we already know and desire to be. That power is available through faith in Christ. God wants us to be better people, more successful in our work, kinder, and more forgiving; and if we believe and will let Him help, He will give us the power to become. It is not something we do simply by ourselves.

Christians are becomers who are growing by drawing on spiritual resources. Keith Miller has written a book with that title: *The Becomers*. It is a good title. We are in the process of developing, and Christian experience is not a matter of arriving at a certain place but of being on a journey toward a goal and becoming children of God.

God through his natural laws of growth has given a little tree the power to become a big tree. He has given a caterpillar the power to become a lively butterfly. He has given a child the power to become an adult, and He has given to those who believe the power to become more Christlike, children of God.

LITTLE DOG—BIG SLED

There is a great story in the fifth chapter of the Gospel of John. A man had been ill for a long time. He had been lying beside a pool where people went for the healing waters. They believed that the first person into the pool when the water bubbled (which happened periodically) would be healed. Jesus came along and talked to the man. The man gave excuses for not having been able to get into the pool. He said there was no one there to put him in when the water bubbled. His negative attitude may have been a part of his problem, but he had been there a very long time and believed in his excuses.

Jesus asked him something very interesting: "Do you want to be healed?" (RSV). That was a good question. Maybe the man had accepted and settled for a life of sympathy and begging and had given up all hope of becoming anything but a beggar. But he said he did want to be healed, and then Jesus did not even bother to put him in the water. Sometimes we miss that in the story. Jesus told the man to pick up his bed and walk. He didn't scold the man for not trying sooner; He didn't punish him for having wasted a large part of his life; but He gave him power to become a person who could do what he had to do. The man believed and was given power to become a more self-sufficient, able person.

After the crucifixion Peter was terribly discouraged and frustrated. In his weakness he had failed and denied his Lord three times. How disgusted he must have been with himself. Judas, who had betrayed his Lord, actually went out and committed suicide. Peter may have considered it. But after the resurrection on the Day of Pentecost, Peter believed what he had been told, and he received power that he had never had before. He received power to stand up for what he believed and to become a great leader and an inspiration to others (Acts 2:14-36).

I know a young woman who by nature is so timid that she has always found it very difficult to speak in public. She is talented and has good things to say, but there is this natural fear of leadership roles and group involvement. I believe many of us have experienced it, and it is not easy to deal with. But for a while her church was without a pastor and needed someone to give some leadership to assure the church's continued life. Believing in this the young woman was given the power to lead some very inspirational worship services and preach some good sermons. She was given the power to overcome her fears and self-consciousness. On other occasions, because she believes very much in an important cause, she has been given the power to become an effective public speaker for outside groups and has been a very important witness for the causes in which she believes. In discussing this she simply said: "I saw my burning bush." Such an experience is not just a matter of making up one's mind and saying, I'm going to be brave. It is finding, through believing, the power to become what you need to be, so you can pull the sled that you know needs to be pulled.

Moses knew that his people needed leadership, that they were hurting. But Moses had a low opinion of himself. He was a sheepherder, not a prince, and he stuttered. When he was asked to lead his people, Moses said he couldn't do it because he couldn't speak well. He wanted the job to go to someone else because he questioned his own ability. But through it all, God over and over gave Moses the assurance that he would be given the power as he needed it, including the help of his brother Aaron who

LITTLE DOG—BIG SLED

was more gifted in speech. A rather ordinary Moses had seen his burning bush and was given the power to become the leader of his people (Ex. 3—4). This can happen in the life of any person. Moses was not a truly outstanding person except through this power that he found through believing that God is for real and would help him do what he was asked to do.

It is good to read in the Scriptures about those people who were given power, but it is also important to remember that the gospel assures us that the power to become is also for us: "To all who received him, who believed in his name, he gave power to become children of God" (RSV). This is for anyone in any situation. Maybe you want to become a better salesperson, more successful in your business, a better teacher, preacher, singer—whatever you can truly feel that you are being asked of God to do. To most of us this will apply to the desire to be a better wife or husband, son or daughter, friend and neighbor. Through believing we can receive power to become more understanding, forgiving, and loving. The burning bush is not just a bush on fire. It is a symbol of God's action, His personal contact with our lives.

When we seek God's power for our lives, we need to avoid the tendency to talk about God instead of talking with God. Too often in grief we will say: "Why did God let this happen to me? Why did God let me lose my job?" Whenever we put it this way we are talking to someone else about God, rather than talking directly with God. This is not communication. If we have a son or daughter, we would much rather have the child come directly to us with a problem rather than going to friends at school or some other relative and asking, "Why did Dad do this to me, or why has Mother acted the way she did?" It is when the child comes and talks directly to us that we can communicate and bridge a gap of misunderstanding that has developed.

I believe God feels the same way. When Jesus faced difficult situations He talked with God, not about God. On the cross He did not cry out and ask: "Why does God allow me to suffer and be crucified?" He cried out: "My God, my God, why hast thou forsaken me?" (Matt. 27:46). And then: "Father, into thy hands I commit my spirit!" (Luke 23:46, RSV). It is in this personal contact that He received power to become victorious even over death.

All of us face big problems. We want to do better than we are doing. God wants us to do better than we are doing. And He wants us to come to Him with the problem so He can give us power to deal with it. Sometimes we are discouraged and frustrated. Sometimes we get a pretty poor opinion of our abilities. We see ourselves as pretty small dogs, and we feel we are hitched to an awfully big and heavy sled. We may cry out saying we just can't handle it—we may even find ourselves turning to bite someone. But we can be sure that God is not bringing out a switch. He is saying to those who believe: "I will give power, not punishment; achievement, not failure; the power to become my children."

18

Frogs and Pollywogs

"The old has passed away, behold, the new has come" (2 Cor. 5:17, RSV).

Among the pleasant experiences of my childhood was my work helping my father irrigate on a typical farm in southern Idaho. In the irrigation ditches there were those wonderful creatures: pollywogs. I began, very early, as I dealt with pollywogs, to be a philosopher and theologian. Pollywogs raise profound questions about life and the way that we and they deal with the problems of an ever-changing world.

In the spring water was turned into our ditches, in the fall it was turned off, and in the winter the ditches were dry. Pollywogs, having tails to swim with but no legs, can only live in water. Yet every spring when the water came, the pollywogs soon appeared. This seemed a miracle. Through the summer they lived in water, depended on the water, and seemed to me to be happy and content. But the ditch would go dry at the end of the summer. What would happen to the pollywogs?

Again a miracle, far beyond the understanding of a pollywog. Just before the ditch went dry the pollywogs would lose their tails, grow legs, and turn into frogs who

113

didn't need water in the ditch. It was an amazing adjustment; it was remarkable timing, just in time to avoid a major crisis, and it seemed to work out even though the pollywogs did very little to bring it about. I suspect it happened even without the knowledge of some of the pollywogs. I doubt if the pollywogs could have improved on the process even if they had tried.

Later in life, when I became more aware of the ways of people, I began to imagine a rather brilliant pollywog that had insights a little beyond the average. He figured out the great truth that the ditch would go dry. He became very anxious about the future of the pollywogs because to him it was obvious, with all the pollywog knowledge that he possessed, that when the ditch went dry, his species would be doomed. In fact, as he saw it, it would be the end of the world.

So he hurried around to all the other pollywogs and tried to get them to organize and do something to save the world from this very gloomy prospect. He had little success. He even became irritated with his fellow pollywogs, and at times he was unpleasant to live with. Most of them were too busy just growing up and trying to be good pollywogs. Some even went so far as to say: "We have plenty of water now, plenty of food; what are you so worried about?"

The problem with this bright pollywog was in his discovery of a great truth but only part of the truth. He knew the water would dry up, but he didn't have enough confidence in the wonder of a Creator who, by the time the water went away, would have made the next step in His work of creation and adapted the pollywogs into frogs—ready for life on land and even their hibernation in the mud in the bottom of the ditch.

The precocious pollywog, like many of us today, did have a great deal of knowledge. We have figured out that some very serious problems confront us in our life in society and on earth. We have some great truths, but often we do not have enough of the truth. We have become so good at creating things, changing our environment, that we sometimes forget that we are still only a small part of the total work of the truly great Creator. So we get uptight and anxious because we really don't know what we are going to do, and we fail to put enough confidence in a God who does know what is going to happen.

We need enough confidence in God so that we can concentrate our major efforts on living good lives, sharing our burdens, loving each other, and lying down to rest in peace when evening comes. There are certainly many aspects of life which, if left entirely to our human wisdom, look pretty gloomy. But so little really depends only on human wisdom. We will do well from time to time to read again some of the great passages from the Book of Job: "Where were you when I laid the foundation of the earth?" ... "when the morning stars sang together?" ... "Where is the way to the dwelling of light?" (Job 38:4, 7, 19, RSV).

We in our time, as every generation has had to do in its time, face some serious concerns. We have discovered some great truths which by themselves paint a gloomy picture of the future. We must add to them the whole truth: God already knows about the problems, cares about this creation, and is taking care of it as He always has and will continue to do. And in our own personal lives, which are our primary concern, if we are not satisfied with what we are, if we long for something better, we need to remember there is a power that can change human nature.

We like to say we can't change human nature, which is true. We can't even change a pollywog into a frog. But God can and does, and this is our hope. When we get concerned and anxious, we need to look about us at the wonder of creation and realize that the Creator of all things is concerned about every concern of yours and mine and every concern of our country and the world. We need to trust more than we do. "Consider the ravens . . . God feeds them. . . . Consider the lilies, how they grow . . . O men of little faith!" (Luke 12: 24-28, RSV).

Sometimes we fail to see what God can do because we try to make things too complicated. Maybe this is what Jesus had in mind when He said we need to become as little children. Once in a while it is good to go and look in a ditch and watch the pollywogs and remember that God has worked out a plan for their future. If He can do that, He can take a person whose life is broken, a person who is discouraged and in despair, and make a new creation. And He can help us adapt to conditions in a changing world.

We all have thrilled at some time to that lovely story of the ugly duckling: the poor little swan who thought she was a duck. What a miserable life she had because she didn't fit in with the ducks. The ducks gave her a hard time. She spent one whole winter in terrible isolation before she came to the realization that she wasn't supposed to be a duck. The great day came when she saw her reflection in the water and could cry out: "I'm a swan, a beautiful, graceful swan. I don't have to worry about being an ugly duck." It is a terrible thing to spoil our lives, living in fear because we forget the greatest of all truth: we are in the care of a Creator who can make all things new. We do not have to carry the whole world on our shoulders. We can trust God to guide us into whatever the future may hold in a very fast-changing world where we don't know what tomorrow will bring politically, socially, or any other way. But we know that God knows, and we can trust Him. He can take us through the terrible winter of doubt, the dark night of the soul, or a period of wondering; and we know there will be a springtime. For us the prospect of atomic war or nuclear winter is as bad as the prospect of a dry ditch was for the pollywogs. But we have access to a faith and a knowledge of God that the precocious pollywog didn't have, and we should not share his extreme pessimism.

For several years we lived in the country of the great horned owl. The great horned owl does what, from a shortsighted point of view, is absolutely stupid. It nests in the coldest part of the winter in February. Often when the temperature was 25 below zero Fahrenheit, we would go out at night and listen to the mating call of the great owls. We knew they were nesting in a frozen world in which there was no prospect of feeding the babies when they hatched. Obviously, the owls had no way of knowing that there would be a way to feed the babies when that time came. An all-wise Creator has endowed the horned owl with an instinct to nest at just that time so that when the eggs hatch, the melting snows of March will uncover a vast source of food for the new family.

So generation after generation the great horned owl nests at a time which, if one were doing it from the point of view of the obvious appearance of things, is ridiculous. But because there is a higher power that guides the flight of the migrating geese, the nest design of the oriole, and the nesting season of the owls, it works out all right.

We can become so anxious about the world in the year 2009 that we neglect our own souls, our own spirits, our own families, our own morals in this current year. If we do our best with what we have this year, we can trust God to do His part when we come to the problems of 2009. If we do our best with the gift of life we have now, and if by then the ditch has gone dry, I believe we will have learned how to live a good life in the grass and reeds along the ditch bank, and we will have legs that will sustain us on dry land.

We are inclined to think that things have to be as they have always been and function in ways our limited minds can always understand. But in a world of constant creation, things never are as they always were. Every new day is just that: a new day and a new creation. This is why one of our deepest needs and basic instincts is our need for adventure. Knowledge is always knowledge of the past and by itself is not an adequate guide to the future. Life is an adventure in faith and hope. Our minds cannot grasp all the implications of nuclear power and space travel. But with faith in a Creator who loves His creation, we can face the future with confidence and our eyes open to the wonder of the world, our hearts open to the wonder of friendship and love, and our minds open to new ideas.

With so many gloomy predictions about the future I

like to remember the pollywogs. With our human limitations we may not be able to ensure that there will always be water in the ditch, but I don't want to give up in despair just at the time we may be losing our tails, sprouting legs, and being prepared to live good lives in situations that are entirely new to us.

19

A Bucket of Muddy Water

"Be still, and know that I am God" (Ps. 46:10).

In spring or early summer I have camped beside mountain streams that were still just a little bit muddy from spring runoff. Often the water as it flows along will look quite clear, and it is only after one has dipped a bucketful for camp use that the small particles of silt or soil still in suspension become evident. When we have not been able to find a spring, and we know that the water is coming from uninhabited areas where there is very little danger of any really serious impurity in the water—only a little good "clean dirt" that is rather unappealing—we have used a lot of this kind of water. With much more use of the out of doors today, by many more people, I certainly do not recommend using such water for drinking without boiling it, but in years past I have used a lot of it with no ill effects.

A long time ago I learned an important lesson. When I dipped up a bucket of slightly muddy water, there was nothing at all that I could do to clear it up. Pouring it carefully from bucket to bucket, stirring it, and even boiling it would not rid it of the unwanted particles. But if I

A BUCKET OF MUDDY WATER

would fill my buckets at night, and just let them sit still till morning, I could then carefully dip out some very clear water. I could see the mud sitting quietly on the bottom of the bucket. The quiet natural force of gravity, which constantly surrounds us and helps us keep things in place where they belong, could pull the unwanted particles out of the water, settle them to the bottom, clear things up, and accomplish a good thing that I could never do by myself no matter how hard I worked at it. In fact, the harder I worked at it the more I muddied the water.

Very often as we deal with the problems that confront us, it seems that life is like a bucket of muddy water. Sometimes tensions build up in our relationships with other people; sometimes our own desires pull us in different directions, and our inner lives are in turmoil. And so often in such situations, the harder we strive the more we stir things up. It is good to know that there is a power as dependable as gravity that constantly surrounds us, that is seeking to hold us steady; a power that can do wonders to clear things up if we will simply acknowledge it, relax, and allow it to act. Surely this is the power that the prophet had learned to rely on when he said: "They that wait upon the Lord shall renew their strength" (Isa. 40:31). Many of life's most difficult problems are made worse by our frantic, hurried efforts to solve them with our own limited means; sometimes our misguided efforts actually cause the problems we are trying to escape.

I remember working with a spirited young horse. He was gentle enough but a bit jumpy and frightened of new experiences. He had been saddled several times and even been ridden a few times. But on a certain day, perhaps when I was in a hurry, I had put his saddle on him and was leading him around a little when something caused him to jump. As he jumped, not really bucking, the stirrups popped him in the ribs. This caused him to jump a bit harder and the stirrups popped him harder still. His next jump jerked the lead rope out of my hand, and, doing the only thing he could think of to solve the problem of the strange popping of the stirrups, he began to run and buck to the best of his ability to try and rid himself of the strange creature on his back that just kept hitting his ribs harder and harder.

Naturally, the harder the horse bucked, the harder he got thumped. He put himself into his do-it-yourself problem solving with such vigor that I feared he would destroy himself crashing into a fence. Stumbling over his dragging lead rope, bucking and running in blind panic, he was a hazard to himself and everyone around him. He did manage to jump one ditch and one fence and get a bad scratch on his leg.

Finally, when he got in a situation where he could buck no more, he stopped. Of course, his torment stopped. The wonderful power of gravity quietly put the stirrups down at his sides where they belonged. When I picked up his lead rope he was still trembling with fear, and as I talked to him and quieted him I told him how silly I thought he had been. But I have to admit that I have sometimes done just about the same thing in regard to some of my own problems that have come up unexpectedly.

In the rural community where I grew up, there was a man who wanted to stop a neighbor's dog from straying onto his property. He caught the dog and tied a rather large tin can to the dog's tail. When the dog found that the can was following him, he began to run to get away

A BUCKET OF MUDDY WATER

from it. The faster he ran, the faster the can followed and banged against his legs. This created real fear and panic that again increased the fruitless effort to outrun the problem.

Fortunately, it was not too far back to the dog's home, and his owner was out in the yard. Trusting his owner the dog dashed up and stopped at his master's feet. Of course, the moment he stopped and sat still, his torment stopped. Without really knowing why, but knowing who he could trust, the dog had done the sensible thing, which was to stop trying to do anything; to be still in the presence of one who could solve the problem and soothe his fears. Sometimes we give ourselves a lot of unnecessary punishment before we are willing to be still and leave our problem at the feet of One who not only can calm a stormy sea but can settle a bucket of muddy water.

Looking back on my own life from the perspective of age, I recall too many times when my own impatience and hurry to solve problems has only made them worse or created new ones. The solution to many problems is like the process of healing a wound. It simply takes time, and the most important thing we can do is leave it alone—picking at it only delays the healing. Those of us who have worked with livestock a good deal know that there are often injuries that respond best to the two great medicines that we call "Father Time" and "Mother Nature."

I remember a fine horse that suffered a serious leg injury. Friends told me there was nothing I could do for it; I would simply have to put her down. About one thing they were right. There was nothing I could do for her. But it was wonderful what the natural processes of healing did for her. I simply turned her out to pasture with good food and rest, and in several months she was completely restored.

The writer of the fortieth Psalm says: "I waited patiently for the Lord; and he inclined unto me, and heard my cry." Possibly the most important word here is *patiently*. Sometimes it takes a while for muddy water to come clear. And sometimes we are so concerned with making things happen that we have a hard time waiting patiently while we let things happen. God is busy even when we are not. God's action in our lives can be like seed that is planted in the ground, that can sprout and grow and mature even while we sleep and go about our daily tasks, although we do not know how God does it.

Often a troubled person coming into my office with a problem will begin by saying: "I'm all mixed up." That is a good description of a troubled spirit and confused goals in life. It is amazing what God can do with a little time of stillness. We are the ones who do the stirring and mixing. God's power can work in ways quite different from our ways. Sometimes just overnight He can settle out the mud and let the water of our lives come clear again.

20

Little Tiger Cat

Little Tiger Cat was an ordinary cat. She was an excellent hunter, an outdoor cat. I have never been especially fond of cats in terms of cuddling them or sharing the house with them. I'm an outdoor person, and I admire and respect an outdoor cat that knows her stuff and does her work well. Tiger was a well-mannered cat; she did have a more personal relationship with our daughter than with me. My relationship with Tiger was based on mutual respect. I've always tried to do my work to the best of my ability, and that is how she did hers. And she did it well.

We had a few horses and a nice little stable. Tiger kept the stable free of mice and rats. Mice and rats can cause a lot of problems in a stable. They chew the strings on the baled hay and cause the bales to break apart when they are moved, and their nests in the hay make the hay foul-smelling and unpleasant for the horses to eat. We often kept rolled grain in sacks, and mice will eat holes in the sacks and cause more grain to be spilled and spoiled than what they eat. With Tiger on the job, we had no problems with mice and rats.

She also did a good job on gophers that were constantly damaging our garden and making holes and mounds in our lawn. Within a year of her taking over the job of guardian of our property, the gopher problem was reduced to an occasional foolish gopher whose attempt to move in was quickly thwarted. She took understandable pride in her work and would report to the backdoor with a gopher, prior to eating it. Apparently she wanted us to know she was doing her work well.

Tiger and I shared a few short and very busy years. It was a busy period in my professional life. She had her work to do and I had mine. I didn't spend time with her though I appreciated her warm relationship with our daughter. I realize that for one who is not a cat fancier, I had a very warm spot in my life for her. I certainly would have done anything I could to keep her from harm; I never would have knowingly hurt her. I never invited her into the house; she never offered to share a mouse with me. We simply respected each other and had a strong bond of friendship.

I shall never forget the day our daughter brought Tiger in from a nearby hayfield. Tiger was not around our yard when Heidi came home from a school, so Heidi had gone to look for her. She found Tiger in a field of new-mown hay—a field where Tiger had been hunting when the mower came along. Her little body was mangled and wracked with pain. She lay trembling and helpless when Heidi found her. She would never hunt again. She was beyond the help of stitches or wonder drugs.

There is something fine about a mower making hay—fresh, clean, sweet-smelling hay. But the result is devastating when a mower touches bone and flesh. Heidi had heard Tiger crying, gently picked her up, and tenderly carried her home. Heidi was a ranch-raised girl, and though quite young, she seemed to understand the extent of the damage suffered by her beloved cat. She cradled Tiger in her arms, gently stroked her fur, and talked to her with words of affection and assurance of her caring.

Being held tenderly by one who loved her seemed to ease Tiger's pain. Somehow she knew she was cared for, knew that her fear and pain were shared. It seemed she cuddled closer into the arms that held her—closer to the body of the one she trusted. She didn't scold, she didn't blame, and she was no longer crying. Now that she had been found and had the reassurance of loving arms around her, she seemed somehow content, even though drop by drop her life blood was dripping away and there was nothing we could do to stop it. In some strange way Tiger knew the struggle was over, but in the loving arms of her owner and her friend it was all right.

As Heidi held Tiger and caressed her, I was leaning close, hoping against hope to find some way I might do more to help her. Leaning close to her I heard something that amazed me. Tiger was purring! I found that tears were running down my face as I listened. Through all this pain she was purring—somehow saying, "It's all right now." And purring softly, in the gentle arms of one who loved her and cared for her, she died.

Many years have passed since the death of Little Tiger Cat. But I shall never forget, and I never want to forget, that picture of trust and assurance that let her die purring—purring with content because she knew she was safely in the arms of the one she trusted even as I hope to trust my God. In the years since the death of Little Tiger,

I have had the experience of an illness that did not seem to respond to medication, and I thought it might well be my own time to walk through the valley of the shadow of death. I thought of Little Tiger and the contentment that she found in the gentle arms holding her close in her time of suffering—the arms that removed her fear and gave her an assurance that let her spend her last moments purring.

It was my good fortune to recover from that illness, to be granted some additional years, but we all know that soon or late, in the wisdom of God, there will come that day when we, through accident or age or disease, will know that our struggle is over. And as people of faith we will have more reason than Little Tiger Cat to know that our hope, our assurance, and our future is in the gentle arms of God who loves us. Though the ones who gather around us may weep, with the trusting confidence of that fine little barn cat, we can enter into our new adventure purring. For we know that "neither death, nor life ... will be able to separate us from the love of God in Christ Jesus our Lord" (Rom. 8:38-39, RSV) and "underneath are the everlasting arms" (Deut. 33:27).